An Heiress of Holocaust | Sarah Segal

Producer & International Distributor
eBookPro Publishing
www.ebook-pro.com

An Heiress of Holocaust
Sarah Segal

Copyright © 2020 Sarah Segal

All rights reserved; No parts of this book may be reproduced or transmitted in any form or by any means, electronic or mechanical, including photocopying, recording, taping, or by any information retrieval system, without the permission, in writing, of the author.

Translation from the Hebrew by Zoe Jordan

Contact: ss8621674@gmail.com

ISBN 9789655752472

To my sister, Rachela.
Thank you for being you.

AN HEIRESS OF HOLOCAUST

HOW MY FAMILY SURVIVED THE HOLOCAUST AND ITS LASTING EFFECT ON MY LIFE

SARAH SEGAL

CONTENTS

Introduction	9
Chapter 1 An Extension of Her	11
Chapter 2 The Black Cloak of the Holocaust	21
Chapter 3 Wysokie Mazowickie, My Shtetl	31
Chapter 4 The Ghetto	47
Chapter 5 Ghetto Liquidation and the Mazura Forest	75
Chapter 6 Zambrow	103
Chapter 7 Death Breathing Down Their Necks	117
Chapter 8 The "Union" and the Rebellion	151
Chapter 9 Confession and Condemnation	163
Chapter 10 Liquidation of Auschwitz	175
Chapter 11 Work and Extermination Camps	191
Chapter 12 A Visit to Wysokie	213
Chapter 13 The Ship That Wasn't Meant to Sail	225
Chapter 14 Where Will I Go? To Whom Can I Turn?	245
Chapter 15 The British Mandate	249
Chapter 16 My Friend Naima	259
Chapter 17 Austerity — Everyone is Hungry	267
Chapter 18 A Glance Back in Anger	289

INTRODUCTION

As the generation of Holocaust survivors leaves our world, it is the duty of the next generation, their sons and daughters, to pass on their personal stories, their experiences and losses over the course of those horrific six years.

I wrote this book in response to growing anti-Semitism, the trend of Holocaust denial, and a concern that the genocide of European Jews will be relegated to our forgotten, distant past along with the Inquisition.

In my book, I tell the story of my childhood in the shadow of my mother, a Holocaust survivor, and how I became her anchor in light of her bipolar disorder. I also tell the story of my family, the weight of whose history

I bear, and how it was affected by that now dwindling generation. In my book I lay out the full account of my mother's experiences and the dark hold it had over her for many, many years.

This book is distinctive in that it sheds light on the plight of my generation on the post-trauma that many of us suffer from our childhoods, in which we experienced, identified with, and suffered the pain of our parents who survived the Holocaust. The book describes the complexity of our lives alongside our parents for whom the pain of the Holocaust never abated and how they unintentionally passed on their personal tragedy to their unsuspecting children.

CHAPTER 1

An Extension of Her

The four seasons of the year always seemed mixed up to me. Autumn preceded summer and spring, always slow to arrive, brought winter along with it. The last gloomy season would refuse to yield its place to the next. Most of the time I didn't know how to function in the turmoil that each season induced within me, but as spring began to bloom, it not only seemed to impose exemplary order in the universe, but also managed to conduct a seasonal harmony that thrummed in my heart all year long.

As a kid, when I got up in the morning, I never knew into which season I had woken. Waking up always felt as jarring as an earthquake. I was ushered into the new day by two arms jerking my body. If that didn't shake off the cobwebs of sleep, my mother would raise her arms and shake her head; the shouting that emitted from the depths of her consciousness would fill the room.

"Get up! You've slept long enough. You are making up for all the hours of sleep that Hitler took from me. I wish I could have slept then, even just one hour, between your starched sheets and luxurious comforter, just one hour! The likes of which I couldn't have even dreamed of."

But I nestled in further and covered my ears. She rattled and shook me relentlessly, this time with renewed vigor. I sat up in bed as though possessed.

"Leave me alone. Don't bring up Hitler first thing in the morning," I said angrily.

But she didn't let up.

"Quit idling. I'll get another note from your teacher saying you aren't concentrating in class. If you hadn't gone to sleep so late yesterday, you wouldn't be ruining your day and my life. What are you listening for, eavesdropping on us talking every night? It's not for you. You have a better life. You children don't need to think about these kinds of things anymore."

"Mama, just five more minutes," I pleaded. She left me and went back to the kitchen. The smell of scrambled eggs reached my nostrils and interrupted my stolen moments of extra sleep. But I didn't get up.

"You should know not to treat me that way first thing,

you should leave me in peace."

There was a sudden outburst.

"You're not up yet? What am I going to do with you?"

I sank into the pillow, sobbing. I knew that Mom couldn't stand my morning tears and she would soften. She leaned toward me, sitting on the edge of my bed, held me and joined in my crying. I felt ashamed and racked with guilt.

How can I do this to her? She suffered so much before bringing me into the world and now I aggravate her from the moment I wake up in the morning, I thought. My heart ached and guilt raged within me.

I suddenly sat up in bed. She gathered me in her arms, planted a wet kiss on both my cheeks, wiped my tears, then her own and said, "Sorry my sweet girl, you know that I only want the best for you."

Energized, I hurried through my morning routine. I put on khaki shorts, fitted on my slim hips, from which my two thin, matchstick legs dangled. I stood before the messy wardrobe and pulled out a white cotton shirt with a flower print — the one from the most recent package of gifts that Aunt Basha would send from America once in a while.

The cup of hot cocoa was already waiting on the table.

I looked at it with disgust. Another morning argument threatened to erupt, upsetting my stomach. My plate was already loaded with omelet. A slice of dark bread heaped with butter only added to my anxiety. How would I manage to get all this food down? I stared at the meal.

"Why aren't you eating? It's eight already! You'll be late for school again."

I dithered with the fork, balancing a few morsels from the heap of eggs. When it was loaded up, I brought the fork toward my mouth, but it fell from my hands and the omelet I had piled onto it scattered everywhere. Mom, busy preparing my sandwich for the morning snack, cried out at the sound of the silverware landing on the floor. "Are you throwing food again?" she cried.

"No, it fell," I mumbled.

Now she knew that I could not be trusted. She stood before my full plate like a policeman. Anxiously, I proceeded to stuff my mouth with moderate portions of egg.

"Eat the bread. It's a shame to waste the butter. For years I didn't so much as taste it. I was happy to be able to get just one slice of bread. But butter? Who could even dream of butter?"

I nibbled at the bread. The butter melted on my tongue. I could feel a wave of nausea rise from my intestines.

Mom savagely grabbed the fork from my hand. She removed the full plate from the table, opened the lid of the garbage can and threw the entire meal, on its dish, into the trash.

I wait for the worst of it. My eyes fill with tears of compassion. Mom's eyes blazed and she blurted, "Fine. At least drink the cocoa. It's gone cold. Do you want me to heat it up for you?"

"Yes," I replied just to buy more time. Maybe it would go the same way as the eggs.

The cocoa returned steaming hot. I never liked milk. Even the cocoa wasn't enough to hide the velvety smell and taste that would slip down my tongue and stick in my throat.

"Now what are you waiting for? You want it to get cold again?"

I closed my eyes, taking sips of the frightening drink. Before it even made it halfway down my throat, nausea flared up. With my hands covering my mouth I ran to the bathroom and released the precious drink into the toilet.

Mom gave in, wiped my mouth and handed me my schoolbag containing a sandwich stuffed with greasy sausage, the kind that Dad would bring home from the delicatessen at the Carmel market. Those kinds of foods always revived the taste of the home that was destroyed.

Every morning, I breathed Mom's horrors from the Holocaust into my lungs. From my earliest childhood, my life was interwoven with the sights, stories and lessons that I had to draw from my mother's bitter experience. At night she would return to the "lager" (concentration camp), beg for her life before the Gentile Chernovsky standing over her, trying to rape her. Her mental illness destabilized me and exacerbated the imbalance in my life. I was an extension of her. Everyone said I looked like her. Yes, I was crazy like her. I hated her, loved her, blamed her and pitied her all at once. When her behavior got completely out of control, Dad would call a taxi. To the sound of her screaming, "I'm not crazy!" and her body shaking with furious resistance, we managed, Dad and I, aged 14, to my great shame at how this might look to my friends and neighbors, to load her into the backseat of the taxi which went from Magdiel to Talbiya, the psychiatric hospital in Jerusalem. Dad and I sat on either side of her, trying to calm her down and assuring her that she just needed a few days of rest and relaxation and we would come back soon to take her home. The cost of the taxi —and the price of shame, anger and the feelings of guilt—burdened my troubled childhood.

The return home and the walk to school the next day were a perpetual terror for me. I felt guilty for assisting Dad in sending my helpless mother away. I didn't know what else to do. One moment I felt that I had done the right thing and the next I thought that Hitler had punished her enough and I had no place adding to her misery. Those repeated events with Mom robbed me of my ability to concentrate. I struggled to read even a line of what the teacher had scrawled on the blackboard. By age 14, miserable in school, I already sensed a kind of helplessness, tension, grief, lack of hope. All I wanted to do was sleep, not learn anything, touch anything. I was filled with sorrow and sadness; I felt that they would be with me forever. I sat there, trying to detach myself, to empty my mind of thoughts, just waiting for the bell that would free me from my dreariness. And at that liberating sound, the melancholy transformed into luminous clarity. My mood changed completely. I was likable to my friends. In the company of those girls, I felt funny, free and light-hearted. When I was with them, the house, the distress, the quarrels between my parents receded. The sun was always shining, and it was as if nothing had happened.

Mom's hospitalization sometimes lasted for many weeks or even months. I missed her. My teachers permitted my absence from school once a week. So I would get on an Egged bus which took me from Magdiel to Ramatayim. There I boarded another bus filled with passengers hurrying to their jobs in Tel Aviv. It was so crowded that I didn't even have to hold onto the leather loop that hung from the bus ceiling, which passengers grabbed onto with every squeak of the brakes by the tired, irritated bus driver. The central station in Tel Aviv was repugnant. On their way, passengers would throw trash, scraps of food, old newspapers and anything they could get their hands on. The smell of steaming falafel, deep-fried and swimming in oil, came from every corner. The stalls were filled with vegetables, citrus fruits and everything Israel produced. The walls of the movie theater, "The Cinema," were covered with huge posters that promised films full of suspense, sex, lust and love. The actors' faces were familiar to me. My friends and I always passed the weekly publication *The Cinema* among ourselves. The girls' eyes would flicker with a look of longing at the sight of the images of Marilyn Monroe, Liz Taylor and others, which inspired our admiration for those we wanted to look like.

But I didn't dally there. I bought a ticket for the bus that would take me to Jerusalem. For that journey, my head empty of thoughts, I stared out at the rocky landscape. At the central station in Jerusalem, I transferred to the final bus of my trip which let me off down the road from the Talbiya psychiatric hospital. Mom was so happy to see me. She looked relaxed and didn't hold it against me that I had taken her to an institution. It was easy to please her. Everything she had here was compensation for what had happened there in the Diaspora, in the Holocaust. Patients in the department where she was hospitalized told me that Mom had had several electric shocks which was why she was so calm. But I didn't believe those crazy people.

My attempts to cope with Mom's illness made me conscious that I was nothing but an extension of her; my life was all mixed up with her disorders. After all, any child of Holocaust survivors will have some symptoms learned from their parents from whom that atrocity claimed so heavy a price. I blamed her for infecting me, for instilling that instability in my life which was full of constant ups and downs. On some of those harrowing nights, when I finally fell asleep, I didn't know what I would wake up to the following morning. The compulsion and attempts to not look or sound like Mom required complete self-supervision over my actions.

The hardest times were when I served professionally as a major in the Israeli Defense Force's (IDF) Military Court of Appeal. Then I had so much responsibility that I could scarcely think about my mother and what she was going through while I was far away. But I managed to repress those thoughts and deal with the many tasks that were required of me.

While I took care of everything, I felt that I was carrying my family history on my shoulders.

CHAPTER 2

The Black Cloak of the Holocaust

Much of life in my parents' home happened under the shadow of the Holocaust. To be the daughter, the second generation of Holocaust survivors is a particular responsibility. Was it a voluntary responsibility or one that was imposed on me? The task I've been given includes bearing the weight, the stories and influences upon that dwindling generation. Clutching the flag of my parents' desecrated honor, I have felt as though I was pushing the wheelbarrow bearing my family's dead toward the pits of mass burial.

Dad never spoke about it; but Mom did. She talked too much. At night I would hear her cry, "He raped me, he raped me," her insufficient Hebrew stuck in her throat. It was years before I understood who "he" and what "rape" was.

"What would I give just to be able to say the word 'Mother,'" she would remind me when I disobeyed her.

My parents' home was like the ember that had survived. It was the candle to illuminate the darkness. The candle which sparked those memories that refused to be forgotten; the candle whose wax has melted but will never be extinguished.

So great was my empathy for their suffering that I felt as though I had been with them every day of the Holocaust. My compassion was always mixed with feelings of guilt that I could not be their life raft and save them from the chaos that had claimed their lives. In my mind, I still contemplate how it was that the lives of my relatives had sunk into those pits. How death sat mercilessly on the back of their necks. Their survival surprises me — the survivors who did not perish are the ones who surprise me.

I feel like I have no existence of my own. I am a symbol, an extension of my parents. In my dreams I see myself in Auschwitz, pulling the cart filled with the dead to the crematorium, into the gaping maw of death. The smoke of the ovens is suffocating, its pungency makes my nostrils flare, inhaling that inhale the scent of scorched flesh. My tears stream from my eyes, put out the burning fire.

Our house is a refuge in the shadow of the Holocaust. In the living room, in a sideboard ornamented with winding wooden carving, there are three drawers. Two are designated for the silverware for special occasions. The third drawer is stuffed with memories. It bears all the weight of those who are no longer among us: their photographs and final letters. The testimony of what was. I knew all of the dead as I knew the living.

Often, when my sister and I were sitting on either side of Mom, she would hold each photo with a kind of reverence and tell its story. This was how I came to know my grandparents, aunts and uncles that I would never meet. She told me how her sister, Cirella, threw her two-year-old daughter Bella from the window of the moving train that was taking them to the concentration camp Treblinka. How the mother had leaped after the baby but was killed by the bullet of a Polish guard. Mom told how the toddler was last seen sitting in the place where she had fallen, while a Polish woman gathered her up into her lap. "You have a cousin in Wysokie Mazowickie who surely survived," she said. "Maybe one day you will manage to find her."

We saw the photograph of 15-year-old Leah, Mom's friend, her eyes looking right at us, her shy smile glimmering. Her red lips reveal a row of bright white teeth. Her chin protrudes with defiance and vitality. Leah, who had not long before been orphaned, her parents transported by train to their certain demise, shared a hiding place with my mother, grandfather and aunts, and other Jews from their town in the attic of the Gentile Slobecki. During the day, while the Nazis combed every corner, overturning the homes of Gentiles suspected of hiding Jews and killing those they found guilty of doing so, Slobecki's wards had to leave their hiding place and find refuge in the tangled forests nearby. At night they were allowed to return to the attic. One day, the Gentile who so desired Leah permitted her to remain in hiding. While the others were in the woods, the Gentile went up to the attic where Leah remained alone and raped her. When the others returned in the evening, they found her clutching her belly and squirming in pain, her virgin blood dripping and soaking into the straw floor of their hiding place. They were beside themselves with rage and disgust, but their frustration and inability to act against the man who was also their guardian paralyzed them. They held Leah to them and protected her from the rapist. Time passed and Leah's belly grew. Her friends did everything in their power to hide her predicament.

One night, the birth pains came, and Leah brought her baby daughter into that bleak, dangerous reality. Leah stifled her pain and her tears, but how could one quiet the cries of a baby just born? Mushka, a childless older woman who was in hiding with them, tore the baby from Leah's arms and suffocated her to death with a pillow. Leah ultimately survived the Holocaust, moved to Israel and married, but she never managed to have another baby.

I knew Leah all my life. I knew her secret, but I never told anybody. I also knew the elderly Mushka. When I was a child, Mom would take me to visit her in the nursing home in Bat Yam where she lived out the rest of her days. But I, knowing the story from early childhood, refused to see her. I was angry; at my young age I did not understand the meaning of what she had done and never forgave her.

In the living room of our house, my parents would often host relatives and friends, most of whom were Holocaust survivors. On those evenings, the conversation would come around to memories, restrained weeping, loss. They would tell one another about their experiences, about the dark past that they could never shake off. Every so often some "uncle from America" would suddenly turn up, bringing presents for us girls, hugging my parents and crying on their shoulders. Those were the more difficult conversations. Facts and stories that were heretofore unknown would appear from the shadows like ghosts. Things were so difficult that my parents, who wanted to protect me from the horrors, would order me to go to sleep. But I was fascinated — I couldn't tear myself away. The desire and the need to know everything were stronger than me. I would hide behind the door and listen to their stories. It was sad and overwhelming, and I would cry in secret. I sensed a kind of intimacy with the Holocaust, as though it were somehow my own private tragedy. Mom would later fill in the blanks and stitch together the fragments that I had heard. In her agitated mental state, she spoke constantly and told me the horror stories. Only from her did I hear the histories of each character who painted my childhood landscape gray; she instilled in me that awareness of suffering and tragedy of my family as well as the other six million victims. I surreptitiously recorded the stories of the survivors and the dead in my diary. I felt it was my duty to document things.

 I am like the memorial candle. My second-generation role obligates me to convey the message of my people.

I feel like we have not yet recovered from the trauma of the Holocaust and I will do whatever it takes to ensure that our Holocaust does not come to rest alongside the forgotten Inquisition. The genocide of the Jews was not another crusade. History is written and rewritten, and I will not let the wheels of time grind the massacre of our people into dust.

Itzik Walman was another survivor. He jumped from a train headed toward the extermination camp Zambrow in North Eastern Poland, only 30 kilometers away from our town. A young Gentile woman, whose husband had worked at our family's flour mill before the war, fell in love with him and gave him shelter in the pit she had dug out for him beneath her kitchen. She gave him a blanket to cover himself and brought food to his hiding place. That was how he survived. Eventually, after the war, Itzik moved to Vienna and grew rich in the gold and diamond business. He took the Gentile woman, who left her husband, along with her young daughter. He housed them, provided for them, and granted them a rich and comfortable life in the city where the idea for Jewish extinction had first been born. Itzik Walman was a close friend of my parents. One day, when I was 10 years old, he visited us in our home in Magdiel. Like a lord, he was driven by a tall, handsome, blond, Arian Austrian driver in a Mercedes that Itzik had had sent from Vienna to the port in Haifa. Itzik stayed in our house but his driver slept in the car. When I grew up, I wondered about the irony of an Austrian guy now serving a Jewish master. I thought how just a few years earlier, Itzik might have been persecuted by his driver or that man's family who may have been members of the Nazi Party.

Later, when I was 19 and I first left Israel for a trip to Europe, I stayed at the home of Itzik, his Polish partner, her daughter and granddaughter in Vienna. Itzik never married her because after all, a Jew should not marry a Gentile woman.

On Sunday afternoons, Vienna's gardens were bustling. I was impressed by the cafes in the verdant parks, the blossoms of spring painting them every color of the rainbow would fill my nostrils with their intoxicating scent, enveloping me with their magic. Women in chiffon dresses, reclining as they were gathered into the arms of their partners, dancing Strauss' waltz. As I was eating a strawberry ice cream, my favorite, and enjoying the Viennese strudel, I was approached by a tall, dark-eyed, dark-haired young Austrian man who invited me to dance. Enchanted, I danced in his arms, my head dizzy from the music being played by the orchestra, by his cheerful smile, the sweep of hair across his forehead fluttering in the wind of the linden trees. Bashful, timid under his piercing gaze that seemed to devour me eagerly, my cheeks flushed. We looked at each other, unable to express the romantic experience transpiring between us. We weren't able to exchange a single word. My Yiddish was too meager to convert into German. English was not yet part of my arsenal, nor his. Just our eyes communicated, spoke to one another. Our silence said it all.

CHAPTER 3

Wysokie Mazowickie, My Shtetl (1936 - 1942)

Poland is a parliamentary republic in Central Europe, bordering Germany to the West, the Czech Republic and Slovakia to the South, Ukraine and Belarus to the East, and Lithuania and the Baltic Sea to the North. Poland's history is a great saga depicting a nation that accepted Catholicism and became a major European superpower. In 1795, Poland was not just the greatest military power in the region, it was also a cultural leader and home to pioneers in various fields such as Frederick Chopin, Marie Curie and Nicolaus Copernicus.

In the 16th century, Poland became home to Europe's largest Jewish population; Jewish immigration was welcomed as it brought skilled and educated manpower, which gave the economic push that the country needed for development during those years. Until the 18th century, Jews made up seven percent of the Polish population and for centuries the two ethnic groups coexisted, peacefully tolerating each other's traditions, religions and ways of life. Jewish musicians, authors and artists made significant contributions to fine arts and added sophistication to Polish culture. They took positions of influence in the fields of commerce, culture, and even politics. Poland was indeed a comfortable home for the Jewish people during this period, even if they were better liked by the nobility than the commoner.

Jews played a major role in industrializing Poland, and the Poles granted them civil rights, ensuring a peaceful life for them. As equal citizens, Jews were recruited into the Polish army and fought bravely in its wars. My father served in the Polish army and the extensive training he went through helped him endure the physical and emotional challenges that awaited him.

Between World Wars I and II, Jews accounted for 10% of the population of Poland, which had become the biggest cultural center for European Jewry.

In the 18th century, Poland was a protectorate of the Russian-Czarist empire and was not yet fully independent. However after World War I, Poland resumed true independence, which it maintained until September 1939, when the Nazis invaded. The tragic end of World War II in Poland constituted the basis for the Soviet-Communist resurrection.

Wysokie Mazowickie

Wysokie Mazowickie was a *shtetl* (a small Jewish town) located in North-East Poland, about 30 kilometers away from Treblinka in one direction, and close to the Lithuanian and Russian borders in the opposite direction.

The small town was established in 1203. In 1492, during the reign of Poland's King Kazimierz IV, the settlement was granted municipal status. In the mid-16th century, ten Jewish families lived there. In 1715, during the war to the north between Czarist Russia and its Polish allies and their enemy Sweden, the Swedes invaded the region and the town was destroyed in battle. Seven years later, in 1722, a synagogue was built from wood with a square shape and a triangular roof. In 1795, after the third division of Poland, Wysokie became a part of the Kingdom of Prussia. The Brok River, a tributary of the Bug River, separated the Jews from the Gentiles.

Intermarriage or close relationships between the two nations were a strict taboo for both populations.

In the heyday of Polish Jewry, the town's economy was based on commerce and skilled labor. Between thirty and forty percent of Wysokie Jews barely got by; only a few were wealthy, like our family, Segal, and the Frumkin family, who were considered to be the town's well-to-do. The Frumkin family was among the richest and most well-connected in the whole region, including Lithuania and White Russia (today's Belarus), and many Jews made their living on their many estates. At that time, there were close trade relations with the Gentiles.

Meanwhile, Wysokie's Jewish population was divided between the Hasidim and their opponents, the Misnagedim, who made up the majority of the community and would pray in the synagogue and the next-door seminary. The Hasidim prayed in *shtiebels* ("little houses") — private homes among which the largest belonged to the Gur Hasidim. In the second half of the 19th century, apart from the Polish majority, our *shtetl* was populated by 500 Jewish households (about 2500 people). There was trade between the two communities. Jews bought agricultural produce from the neighboring Gentile farmers and sold them small industrial products and crafts.

Jewish workshops were small and employed a maximum of two or three apprentices. They sold garments, kitchen items and work tools that they produced. The Jewish community also included vegetable and fruit sellers, shopkeepers, traders of grain, trees and horses. There were also craftspeople such as tailors, watchmakers and glass cutters. Since the closest train station to Warsaw was in the town of Szepietowo, one kilometer away from Wysokie, there were also Jews making their living transporting goods by horse-drawn carts and delivering them to shopkeepers.

Rivka

If I had known what had happened to Rivka, my father's younger sister, I might have understood why every evening, as he sprawled in his armchair in our living room, he stared, unable to draw his eyes away from the ever-present photograph on the wall before him. The photo was of Rivka at age 19, her black hair parted on the side and running down her long neck to her shoulders, a carefully combed lock curling across her forehead. The gaze of her almond eyes was tinged with sadness, but still something of her astonishing beauty came through.

Dad sat, his eyes as blue as the depths of the ocean, their elusive color growing dark and misty. I never saw another set of eyes so blue that they were almost black. His pupils seemed switched off, as though the curtains had been drawn. Moisture filled them around the sides. The muscles of his face did not move, a burning pain turned them to stone. His brown hair hung from his forehead and he appeared very attentive as though he were still taking refuge in the forest, lying in wait for the Nazi who might discover him. There were sometimes tough evenings in our home, evenings when Dad was frantic, hysterical. Although the worst of it was long behind him, the memories of terror still drew him in. An uproar raged within him, the creases in his face illuminating another aspect of Jewish destiny.

I recall one wintry evening when I was 14 years old in 1960 in our little community of Magdiel.

Outside, hail is battering the shutters of the porch off the living room of our apartment. To the sound of brakes screeching, an Egged bus bursts into the bay of the bus stop across from our house, bringing with it a jet stream of murky water that drains away, streaming quickly toward the gutters. The cascade washed the street clean. Wet passengers huddle up against one another under the bus station's little tin roof, their umbrellas dripping water, their thick yellow rubber raincoats protecting them from the piercing cold. At home, Dad leans toward the oil stove, cozying up to the heat of its flames. Metal mesh sits on top, on which hot chestnuts are scattered. Their smell and the crackling sound is like baby chicks emerging from their shells. Each one pierces a hole in my heart. Without even turning to face me, Dad hands me the hot treat that scorches my fingers and burns my heart with pity for him.

Dad dresses in dusty khaki clothing. Bits of wheat and grain accumulate in his pockets and the folds of his pants. The change in his pockets is always full of grain remnants. Everywhere he goes, he leaves dust markings behind him.

I don't like Dad's look. His khaki clothes don't look like the khaki uniform of Moshe, Shula's dad whose shoulders are decorated with the stripes of an IDF artillery officer. I would at least like to see my father in the kind of formal dress worn by Shalom, my friend Miriam's dad. His shirt is always white, his collar always starched. Shalom is a clerk at the local post office. Anything would look more respectable than the dust that covers my father's body when he comes home tired, his eyes dark, from the animal feed supply warehouse that he owns in Magdiel.

Every morning on his way to work, he gets on his bicycle with a clothespin tucked in the hem of the left leg of his pants so that it won't get caught in the pedals. At his feed warehouse, the sacks are stacked one on top of the other: oatmeal, wheat, barley, sorghum, ground carob, seeds and various other grains. Dad's body is bent over with the weight of the sacks he carries on his back. He inserts a pitchfork into each bag to check its contents. Then he loads the sacks onto a wheelbarrow and pours their contents onto the warehouse floor until a small heap forms. With a shovel he then blends the mixture, piles and pours its contents into sacks, sorted according to the names of local farmers, communities or districts to which they will be sent to market. This heavy load is compounded by the added six years of suffering through the Holocaust and its consequent loss and grief.

It used to be different. In the past, in Wysokie Mazowickie, our family owned a flour mill. At harvest time, the Polish farmers would gather the harvest from the fields and bring their crops to our flour mill for grinding. The family factory, at the edge of the town, provided the flour with which to bake bread for the entire district. The mill's wheels also provided electric power to all of the surrounding towns and villages. In those days, our family was among the richest in the region; we had a place of honor in the community. Even when the Nazis imprisoned all of the town's Jews behind ghetto walls, the Segal family remained on its estate in order to provide the essential needs that served everyone, including the Nazis. If I had seen Dad in those days, my heart would have filled with pride.

In Magdiel, as we passed cold, rainy winter evenings, Dad was often trapped in his thoughts. Sometimes friends and relatives came to visit. Then Dad's mood grew happy and cheerful. He loved those evenings, getting together with his family and old friends: those who had come from Poland and risen, as if from the underworld, found my parents in frantic searches, running between various offices to seek out relatives in the 1950s. They turned over every stone until they found their lost relations. A few of the uncles, aunts and close friends had now returned, weary from the war years, to our table packed with the Polish appetizers that Dad bought for them in the Carmel market in Tel Aviv. Throughout long evenings of vodka-infused tears, they would share, each in turn, the terrible things they had experienced.

In the Spring, as we inhaled the pungent aroma of citrus flower buds from our yard, my family celebrated a 1960's Passover seder. On the table, set according to Jewish tradition, we sat around the table with the family of Leibl Frost, a beloved friend of my parents. In Mom's steaming chicken soup, floated the soft, airy *kneidlach* (matzah balls) that she made so well. The *galareta* — a jelly made of chicken cartilage thickened with gelatin and dipped in lemon juice melted in my mouth. Mom had removed the bones from the carp, which only hours earlier were still swimming in the aluminum tub on our balcony, ground up their flesh and turned them into the traditional gefilte fish. With its light color and sweetish flavor, it was served alongside grated horseradish, reddened with beets, the sharpness of which made my nostrils flare until they inhaled the aroma of exile with which they were imprinted. Eagerly, I slid a piece of the gefilte fish dipped in horseradish onto my tongue and suddenly my mouth lit up as if on fire. I leaped to my feet to try to extinguish it.

"Very good," Dad chuckled. "Now we'll have some

quiet from you."

Without responding to his challenge, I dipped a piece of sweet, fluffy challah, braided and sprinkled with poppy seeds, in the fish sauce which melted deliciously in my mouth.

All of the delicacies were served atop the service — a set of fine white porcelain vessels, whose edges were decorated with a gold stripe that accentuated their prestige. The plates were placed one on top of the other, sorted by size and the order of the courses that would be served on them. This was the fancy dishware that my parents had brought with them in a large, wooden crate when they immigrated to Israel in 1950. The festive silverware, and fragile crystal and porcelain were wrapped painstakingly in down comforters. With their elegant design they symbolized Polish wealth and the commercial success that Dad and his brothers had achieved in the four years since the end of World War II, when they emerged from that hell, the loss and the torture of mind and body. They had set up an oil factory in Wroclaw and rebuilt themselves.

After a long break, still sitting at the table, Mom served a fluffy sponge cake made of egg whites, along with tea poured into little glasses that rested inside silver frames, engraved with bold shapes and fancy decorations. The frames served not only as ornamentation but also to keep the tea hot.

At the end of the meal, the lace tablecloth was removed. Wine stains were cleaned with stain remover. The two wooden extensions of the table, which doubled its size, were removed from their tracks and from the wooden grooves where they were bolted underneath the table, folded and returned to their place in the *boydem* — the cave-like storage space above the dining room ceiling. They would remain there, waiting patiently until we celebrated the next Passover, when they would be used again. The table was cleaned with a damp cloth and returned to its normal spot in the middle of the dining room. Tomorrow its prestige would be revoked, and it would resume its role accommodating our daily, non-holiday meals.

The heavy meal tired us out and, as the rest of the guests, their bellies full, went to bed, Dad and I went out to the balcony to inhale the scent of the citrus blossoms. Dad, who was "drunk" from the amount of nonalcoholic Manischewitz wine he had been drinking, (this is sweet wine, essentially juice for children), gave free rein to his memories, those which until that day he had tamped down to the depths of his soul and didn't dare share with his children.

Since that day we have talked a lot about that bloody time. About the traumatic experience that our family and all of Europe's Jews went through. From him I learned the stories of the uncles, aunts and close friends — the approximately thirty Holocaust survivors who were a big part of my young life. Dad let out a heavy sigh, and without me prodding, he began his story:

"Our town, Wysokie Mazowickie — that holy community was wiped out under God's sky," Dad began.

On December 14, 1936, when Dad was 22, three days before the Jewish new year, an atmosphere of tension and fear of impending disaster prevailed among the Jews. And indeed, that morning, our town was struck by young foreigners who roamed the market square sowing their terror and violating the town's tranquility. At three in the afternoon, a sharp whistle was heard, marking the onset of the riots. A group of wild Cossacks — young Russian hooligans — joined them. On their way to the town they blew up bridges and factories beside the train station, blocking the entry of traders' carts loaded with shoes, clothes and all the wares that were on their way to be sold in the market. The Cossacks cut the harnesses of horses from the Jewish wagons and pushed them into a swamp. They stabbed Jewish shop owners to death and robbed the valuable items from among their wares. The hooligans overturned stalls heaped with goods that Jews had prepared for their holiday feast, mixing them all up into a paste that created a nauseating medley of precious foods. They also blocked entry into the Jewish stores, preventing the anticipated sales in advance of the holiday evening. Looting and chaos prevailed. In the main street, a huge, lit-up notice was posted that declared, "Those who buy from Jews are traitors."

Outside the butcher shop, the Jewish butcher had placed cages containing around two hundred chickens meant for the holiday tables. The rioters threw the cages on the ground, let the fowl out one after another and wrung their necks with sadistic pleasure. When they had finished demolishing the market, the hooligans went to Jewish homes, desecrating them and wreaking havoc on everything; they robbed their belongings, destroyed their property, broke their windows and left their homes stripped bare, exposed to the cold wind, and finally, on fire. Most of the Gentile Polish homes that were built from wood and their straw roofs also went up in flames. The Ukrainian Cossacks' bullets whistled overhead. Jews fought the rioters with sticks but could not hold them back.

Hundreds of Jews fled to the deep canal that stretched for about a kilometer through the fields of the Polish fritz. When the clashes were over and the survivors emerged from the canal, they were dumbfounded to see that their town had been completely burned to the ground. Dad came out of his hiding place in the canal to the bright, sun-lit street. The street was empty and silent, but on the sidewalks and in the gutters, he saw the corpses of people he had known all his life.

Later, they learned that during those hours, while the hooligans celebrated their revenge on the Jews, the Polish Gentiles stood by, along with the police officers, enjoying the scene. And so a deep rift formed between the two sides. The Jews were in disbelief and became a target for the gentile hatred which had stirred up the peaceful town.

"Hit the Jews and save the Poles," proclaimed the rioters. In the town's church, the pastor stood before his congregation and ordered that no one buy from Jewish stores. The mayor of Wysokie forbade his citizens from entering into trade with Jews. "Poles buy from Poles," he declared, and "Go back to Palestine," the Gentiles taunted.

Dad sighed deeply. "As a youth I already understood that we had no place in this hostile environment, but where could we go?" he asked. Europe was consumed by hatred for the Jews, which paved the way for the Nazis who arrived at its doorstep three years later. Meanwhile in Israel, desert sands choked the inhabitants and the malaria epidemic, alongside the British Mandate, made it hard for Polish Jews to immigrate to Israel.

CHAPTER 4

The Ghetto: August 3, 1941 to November 2, 1942

On August 23, 1939, Germany and the Soviet Union signed the Ribbentrop-Molotov Pact. The pact included a hidden appendix concerning the division of Poland between Nazi Germany and the Communist Soviet Union, along the Curzon Line, Poland's proposed eastern border that the British had suggested in 1919 at the end of World War I.

This agreement also included the promises from both sides — Germany and the Soviet Union — not to attack each other for ten years. The two powers divided Poland's territory between them. Hitler wanted to take advantage of the country's national resources. In addition, Poland also served his settler colonialism ideology of *lebensraum* ("living space"). The Ribbentrop-Molotov

Pact made it possible for Hitler to go to war first against Poland, and afterward against France and Britain. Under German occupation, there were many zones belonging to the Soviets. Our town, located in Eastern Poland, bordered on Lithuania, which Russia had annexed to Soviet control. The pact did not ease the feeling among the Jews of the town that something terrible was going to happen, but no one imagined that this would be the start of the Jewish people's greatest tragedy. Nobody knew that this agreement would bring about the end of most of European Jewry.

It seemed evident that in signing this agreement, Hitler, the clever manipulator, managed to deceive his rival Stalin into complacency since, with that pact, Stalin was able to relax without fear of a surprise invasion of Poland by Hitler.

Not eight days had passed since the signing of the agreement when, on September 1, 1939, in blatant violation of the pact, Germany invaded Poland and in so doing, marked the beginning of World War II. During the war, the Luftwaffe, (the Air Force of the Third Reich), dispatched one thousand three hundred Messerschmitt fighter jets alongside two thousand Panzer tanks as well as heavy artillery, to conquer Poland and turn its land into an incinerator and a tomb. Though heroic, the Polish army with its outdated weaponry was drastically inferior. The lack of wireless devices in the Polish army did not allow communication between its units and the battle was disastrous. The outmoded Polish army collapsed within several days and, after the heavy barrage on Warsaw, the capital fell on September 27, 1939. To uphold Poland's integrity, the United Kingdom and France declared war on Germany. (The German invasion of Poland was the official reason for the outbreak of World War II). Nevertheless, they did not manage to save Poland.

Suddenly, on September 10, 1939, four days before the Jewish new year, the Nazi armies were already at the entrance to our town. Wysokie was conquered without opposition. The first rounds of gunfire echoed at two in the afternoon. A Polish-German battle took place in the nearby village of Golasze. In its vicinity were railway and bridge projects which the Germans bombed in order to sever regional transport and communications. Tongues of flame rose in the sky, spread everywhere and began to consume Wysokie and its nearby towns. Homes were hit by incendiary bombs and burned up completely. Once burned, they collapsed, their ruins gobbling up Jews and Gentiles alike.

By five in the evening, Wysokie was in ruins. The 18th-century cemetery was destroyed and never rebuilt. Our family's estate, with its flour mill on the edge of town, remained untouched by the battle.

Hundreds of the city's inhabitants roamed the fields all night, fleeing the fire that had taken hold of everything. Others fled with just the clothes on their backs to fields and forests between Wysokie and nearby villages and lost their lives on the way. Some found refuge in the towns of Sokolow, Zambrow and Bialystok. Many escaped and burrowed into the deep canal on the fritz's estate. Belongings that were left behind and survived the fire were plundered.

The next morning, the town was unrecognizable. One surviving radio receiver reported on the intense fighting between the Germans and the feeble Polish army, their fighting power reduced, and of the Germans' progress and the Polish army's retreat. Our town was unarmed and defenseless. Wysokie Mazowickie surrendered unconditionally to the satanic forces.

One day, the Nazis came after Samuel Greenberg, who had in the past served as the Chief of Police and treated everyone with respect and impartiality. During his tenure, Greenberg had given shelter in his home to a wealthy Polish farmer — Dolongovsky — who had gotten entangled in criminal matters. Fearing the Germans, Greenberg had fled from his village of Rika to Wysokie. Later, when the Nazis removed him from office and pursued him, Greenberg asked Dolongovsky to repay him by letting him hide in his home. But the Polish farmer, who remembered Greenberg's kindness, turned him in to the Nazis. Greenberg was taken to the city of Zambrow, where he was killed.

Not two weeks had passed when, on September 12, 1939, the Nazis ordered Wysokie women and children to leave town no later than the following day at three o'clock in the afternoon. The deportees, with only the clothes on their backs, tried their luck in the neighboring town of Bialystok. Since their industries were needed by the Nazis, my father's family was allowed to remain to continue producing electricity and flour.

With the departure of the deportees, the Nazis ordered all the Jews that remained in town — men, Jews and Polish Catholics alike, aged 17 and up, some two hundred Jews and seven hundred Poles — to gather in the church yard. With their weapons pointed at the backs of their victims, and with shouts of "Heil Hitler," the SS soldiers brutally pushed the men into the church, whose capacity was in no way suited to the terrible crowding within. The detainees were held without food, water or air for two days. When the Nazis finally opened the church doors, hundreds of corpses piled at their feet. Jews that survived the suffocating experience were forced to line up while SS soldiers and the gendarmerie — the Polish police force — passed on both sides, banging their heads. Wysokie's mayor was called over. From among the line, he extracted Jewish craftspeople: tailors, shoemakers and those whose professional skill might serve the needs of the occupying army. The rest, exhausted and helpless, were marched thirty miles, the elderly shot to death along the way, to the Zambrow concentration camp, which the Nazis had intended as a transit station until the Final Solution for European Jews at Auschwitz.

Before the Holocaust, my father's family numbered seven people: his parents — Sarah and Fischel Yeruham, my father's brothers Mishka, Yehoshua (Shia) and Haim, his sister Rivka and himself. Mishka, the eldest brother and a road engineer, was kidnapped even before the war by Soviets to serve in the Red Army and spent his entire life in Siberia. There in the snow, he paved roads and built infrastructure for the Red Army, which was how he survived the Holocaust. But because of the Iron Curtain over the Soviet Union, the brothers never met again.

Although the town was devastated in battle, my father's family's large home and factory were undamaged by the explosions. But the privilege given to them in the past—to remain on their estate and continue producing power and flour—was eventually denied them and they were thrown in with the rest to live within the impossibly restrictive walls of the Jewish Quarter. Back in the ruined city, some ten Polish families took over the house. The Nazis also converted the remaining rooms into their local headquarters.

In accordance with the division of land as stipulated by the Ribbentrop-Molotov Pact, on September 26, 1939, the Third Reich withdrew from Polish soil, and our region was handed over to the Red Army, so days began to be better for us. The Russians released the detainees from prison and forced labor camps and let the deportees and those who had fled to nearby towns return to Wysokie. Slowly, the citizens began to return to their homes, most of which had been damaged or destroyed by the Luftwaffe bombings. Road traffic was moving freely again. Germans were no longer seen around, except by the Jew Sukhovolsky, who was shot by a retreating German on his way home. The Soviets helped the town's Jewish inhabitants rehabilitate. For those whose homes were damaged, the Russians provided a note addressed to the Gentile who traded in lumber which enabled them to receive a supply of tree cuttings, for a fee, to be used to rebuild their homes. For those whose homes were entirely destroyed, the Soviets built wooden huts. The Jewish professionals returned to their work and some were employed at the offices of the Soviet authorities which had opened up in the town. The Russians even founded a school for Jewish children, although its teachers were Russian. Jewish youth were recruited to the Red Army and some worked in fortifications. Life was beginning to return to normal. The days passed and already there were 1,100 Jews who had returned from exile living in Wysokie.

Then one Saturday night, a dance was held at the city's Polish school. As the youth were celebrating, Luftwaffe planes began to circle above them. The Russians tried to calm everyone, saying that they were only doing flight exercises, until the Nazi planes began shelling and destroyed the airport that the Red Army had built near the town of Vorobla. It was clear that the Germans were invading once again.

So it was that on June 22, 1941, at two in the morning, after a Soviet rule of less than two years, Hitler once again violated the Ribbentrop-Molotov Pact and the Third Reich's Wehrmacht, their armed forces, invaded the Soviet Union. And so began the bloody Barbarossa Operation. On June 24, 1941, the German tanks reached Wysokie Mazowickie once again. This time they maintained military bases in the Mazura region, to which our town belonged.

A downpour of leaflets, written in Polish, were scattered by enemy planes and called upon the Jews to remain in the town while promising that they would not be harmed. But as always, the Germans did not keep their promise.

With the Nazis' return to our region, their governance was crueler than ever. They imposed harsh orders depriving Jews of their basic human rights. They were not allowed to walk on the sidewalks or to slaughter animals for meat according to kosher practice. Men were required to shave off their beards. All Jews were required to wear the yellow badge on their clothes with the word "*Jude*" printed on it and trade and traffic restrictions were imposed on them. Within several days the persecution and torture of the city's Jews grew. Murders, looting, abuse and forced labor became commonplace. Houses went up in flames and Jewish men were deported to the surrounding villages and towns. Every morning, Jews were required to stand in the church square, where they were put through a series of sadistic abuses. Many Jews were arrested, accused of being Communists. Shimon Tanenbaum was such a suspect and the Nazis executed him through hellish torture. Men, women and children gathered daily in front of the church for forced labor in removing stones and paving the roads that were destroyed by the German Panzer tanks when they invaded the town on September 10, 1939.

On June 26, 1941, a Nazi soldier arrested Leib Weizheva for the misdemeanor of buying an animal. As punishment, he was sent to the city of Lomza where he was shot to death. All at once, the town had changed. There were no more merchants at the market, no more butchers, craftspeople or shopkeepers. There was nobody outside. Everywhere, it was as silent as the grave.

On August 15, 1941, the Jews were ordered to gather in the market square. Panic took hold of everyone; they understood what this gathering meant. Some of the Jews fled but most of them did as they were ordered. An SS officer and a German commissar were already waiting for them in the square, accompanied by Wysokie's mayor and the Polish gendarmerie. The mayor selected tradesmen from a list: shoemakers, tailors, and others who were needed by the Nazis to run the town. The rest of the town's Jews remained where they were, under heavy guard, for the "sanitary committee" that was coming from the city of Lomza in order to sort them, according to their physical state, to carry out various tasks. The Jews were held in the market square for a full twenty-four hours, until, at seven in the morning the following day, they were told that due to disruptions in transportation, the "committee" visit had been canceled. Later they found out that the "committee" had been busy holding an Aktion — a Germans sorting Jews operation — in another town, which delayed their arrival to Wysokie. That was how Wysokie's Jews were saved from the Aktion that had been planned for them. For a while, no mass Aktion was carried out in the town — but from time to time the Germans carried out occasional Aktions, in which they selected those fit for hard labor. The rest of the town's residents, the children and the elderly, who were of no use to the Nazis, were executed.

When the Poles began to cooperate with the Nazis, they "poured oil onto the fire of Jew-haters." The gendarmerie was mobilized for this purpose. The Nazis, who had difficulty distinguishing who was Jewish based on appearance (apart from Orthodox Jews) were now getting assistance from Polish informers, the "Szmalcowniks," and who rushed to point out and reveal their victims. Now was the Polish Gentile's chance to bully his neighbor. The abuse was so unbearable that the heads of the Jewish community themselves appealed to the Nazi occupiers asking to be removed from the hostile environment.

Oftentimes the abuse by the Poles was drastically more severe than that of the Germans. From the Jews in neighboring villages, the town's Jews learned that there they had already established ghettos which prevented the Poles from entering its walls, and as a result there was less abuse and cruelty, so the leaders of the Wysokie Jewish community appealed to the Nazi occupiers to set up a ghetto for them as well.

In August of 1941, the Nazis fenced in three of the town's streets with a barbed-wire fence and thus the ghetto was erected. The ghetto stretched from the Jakobi family home to the Bialsky house, where the main gate stood. The fence continued along the Mystki Road, between the house of Vroebl the shoemaker to that of

Aharon Lazer the carpenter, where the second gate was. The fence ran the length of and surrounded the *rynek* or market square, and the third gate was placed on the main road, beside the butcher shops. The fourth gate was beside the bridge of Mordecai the blacksmith. Even the left side of the Lower street was within the ghetto, while the right side of that street was outside of it. The old Jewish cemetery was also within the bounds of the ghetto. Although my family's home and factory were at the edge of the town, this time the Nazis did not spare us, and we were thrown into the tiny, crowded ghetto. Some ten Polish families, people who had previously been employed in our flour mill took over our house. The Catholic Poles, whose homes were now within the bounds of the ghetto, were transferred to the homes of displaced Jews. A few of the Germans in the city stayed in the Kapitovsky house which was near the road that led to the neighboring town of Szepietowo. The ghetto included some of the town's oldest homes, and refugees leaned on rusting, dilapidated balconies, their eyes anxiously scanning what was going on in the street.

In the course of being beaten and tortured, my father and his friends who were fit for work were sent out of the ghetto on a daily basis to do hard labor. They were separated from their relatives who remained in the ghetto by many kilometers, at the mercy of the Nazis and their Polish collaborators. Children and adults alike were given equally brutal work. Transport in the ghetto was reduced to two carts and horses, which were used by Judenrat representatives to bring bread to the road workers. This was also how food was brought from the nearby villages and wood from the forests. Life conditions in the ghetto grew worse from one day to the next. The Jews lived under constant fear for their lives. When they went to bed at night, they didn't know if they would live to see another day.

Leaving the bounds of the ghetto was completely forbidden unless its occupants were taken to hard labor. But Dad and his brother Haim developed a strategy and even although they had to risk their lives, they were able to bring home a little food. They would bribe Yitzek, the Polish gendarmerie soldier who was in charge of guarding the ghetto's northern gate. As they made small talk with him, the brothers plied him with vodka. Soon enough his nostrils faced the sky and they were able to get out, walk to the nearby villages and bring back some food.

The ghetto became a small state unto itself, trapped

between the barbed-wire fences, among the ruins and rubble remaining from the Nazis first invasion on September 10, 1939.

In time, the Nazis forced 1,350 more Jews into the ghetto from a transport from the nearby towns: Jablonka Koscielna, Kolaki Koscielna, Dabrowa, Wituneg, Kalisz, Wishianeg and Tatra. By Autumn 1941, the ghetto already numbered more than 3,000 people. It was so overcrowded and uninhabitable that its prisoners were beginning to lose their humanity. Members of the Polish militia in blue and white berets were posted at the gates and along the ghetto's streets. Black-uniformed Germans, SS soldiers, ruled the ghetto. The Nazis also appointed Jewish guards and made them responsible for guarding the area between the ghetto walls. The Nazi authorities ordered the Jews to choose a "Judenrat" (in Yiddish: 'Rescue of Jews'), a committee that would represent them before the Nazis. There were thirteen such representatives looking out for the interests of the Jewish community and responsible for implementing Nazi commands. My grandfather, Fischel Yeruham Segal, was one of them. The other twelve representatives were: Rabbi Alter Zak who was appointed chairman of the Judenrat, his daughter the doctor, Golda Zak, Avraham Hertz, Meir Meizner, my father's cousin, Bezalel Tanenboim, Hersch-Yitzhak Trastovacz, David Mauser, Eliyahu Wensover, Bernholtz, Pesach Skovronek, Yaakov Melnik and my grandfather — my mother's father, Shmuel Izak Yalen. My aunt — my mother's sister — Chaya Yalen served as the Judenrat secretary. The Germans even established a Jewish militia within the ghetto which included Shmuelka Susana, Hershel Zilberfenig and Pesach Dalangwicz. Moshe Berner and Vidal Zak were appointed as their commanders. A Jewish police force was also appointed, which worked in collaboration with the Judenrat members and was also trusted to keep the peace within the ghetto. The Judenrat was also in charge of supplying the Nazis with workers and distributing them among various jobs. The members were required to supply around two hundred and fifty workers a day for jobs such as paving the Bialystok-Warsaw road and cutting wood in the forest. During the harvest season, Jews were employed by the fritz from Shepetovka for harvest his crops. In return they received agricultural produce from him. The shoemakers, tailors, furriers, carpenters, metalworkers and others were given licenses to work. Those who worked in the nearby villages could buy goods from the Polish peasants. The Judenrat and the Jewish police organized a soup kitchen for the poor.

Every day, the Judenrat had to provide the Germans with at least 250 workers for forced labor. At dawn, the men were taken from the ghetto and marched some twenty to thirty miles to their workplace while the Nazi policemen, bearing clubs, supervised and hit them for every offense, no matter how small. The Jewish police force also supervised the road work but treated the workers with respect. The Jews mined huge rocks and without any tools, lifted them to the crusher, removed stones, pulverized and crumbled them into gravel, and scattered it on the pits and potholes that remained from the September 10, 1939 Luftwaffe bombings. They also removed the debris all around, repaired the damaged roads and prepared them for use by the Wehrmacht. The Germans ordered them to demolish the old intercity roads and pave new asphalt ones. They were the ones to pave the new road from Zambrow via Tiktin (Tykocin) on the way to Bialystok, and from there all the way to Warsaw. Others were occupied blasting marble tombstones in the Jewish cemetery. The marble stones that were uprooted from the town's Jewish graves, desecrating the honor of the dead, were used by the Nazis to pave the city's sidewalks, but, ironically, the Jews were forbidden to walk on those sidewalks. Some of the workers were men whose weakness and physical condition were not up to the strenuous effort required. These men would be taken out of their ranks by the Nazis and sentenced to death. Their friends tried to cover for them, hid them and, with great difficulty, carried out their work to make up for their inability to complete their tasks. Only a few tradespeople made their living at their profession, but any money they made was handed over to the Judenrat. Over time, and in order to increase output, Jewish laborers from the nearby towns were added to the Wysokie labor force. After 12 hours of debilitating work, the laborers would receive a meal of 220 grams of bread, a bowl of some murky concoction considered soup or, alternatively, coffee. This situation continued until September 1942.

Even though members of the Judenrat risked or even gave their lives to defend other Jews, this did not prevent conflict arising between them and their community. Jews in the ghetto found it hard to balance the Judenrat members' concern for the community with the benefits and luxuries granted them because of their status with the Nazis. After all the Judenrat were the ones who determined who would go to forced labor and who would have to rot within the impossible walls of the ghetto, whose property would be confiscated, who would be given a license to work outside the ghetto, and other such influential decisions.

In the feudal system, Jews were employed as packers in the yards of the Polish landlords. Jewish messengers gathered the potatoes which also constituted their own slave wages. During the hard days of winter, when young Jews were sent to the forests to gather wood to heat the Nazi residences, they were permitted to pull up rotten tree roots and bring them back to the ghetto for heating and cooking purposes. There was no electricity in the ghetto, so oil and candles were used for heating and lighting.

Although it was forbidden, the Judenrat took care of distributing food to the Jews who worked in isolation, at a great distance from their brothers, since the Nazis didn't bother to bring them food at all. The Nazis also appointed Jews to the ghetto police force whose job it was to keep the peace.

The Poles continued to abuse the Jews. Sometimes they were even worse than the Nazis. On one cold winter morning, a Polish police officer uprooted a Jewish family from the ghetto and took them to the Jewish cemetery, where fresh graves had been prepared for them. Their five-year-old daughter turned to the Pole with tears in her eyes. "Sir, you also have a daughter my age, please don't kill us." Without hesitation, the man shot the girl and her family and put them in the mass grave he had dug.

For a while, the Nazis avoided carrying out Aktions, but they executed many Jews for what seemed to them punishable offenses, such as the buying or selling of cattle. In desperation, about five hundred of the town's Jews fled and scattered among the nearby villages or roamed the nearby forest.

One summer evening in 1941, refugees from nearby towns arrived in Wysokie, saying that Nazis were shooting and killing Jews. The town's rabbi and head of the Judenrat, Rabbi Alter, went to the Polish fritzes in the towns of Szepietowo, Szczecin and others and asked them to take the Jewish youth to work on their estates. Upon their agreement, a group of fifty youth, joined by a shoemaker, set out to work. The rest of the men worked in primitive quarries without cranes to lift the rocks. The mining, crushing and the removal of the gravel was done manually. The Judenrat would bribe the German guards with a pair of boots, fabric or meat so they would not abuse the workers.

Many times, Rabbi Alter tested the limits with his assertiveness toward the Nazis. Perhaps on account of his charisma and authority, the Nazis turned a blind eye to his impudence rather than punish him. The rabbi had a dedicated helper, Abraham Hertz, who served as a contact between the Germans and the Judenrat. He was the one who gave the Nazis their gold quotas, books and other assets they demanded of him. But Hertz was unable to stand the harsh tasks he was assigned. He died of heartbreak in the summer of 1942.

In August of 1941, the first Aktion took place — a series of violent acts in the name of sorting the Jews for different tasks. The Aktion was carried out with impeccable order, using the branched logistics that the Nazis invented to send the Jews who had survived until now to their deaths.

Fifteen hundred Jewish men were called to the church yard. Wysokie's mayor pulled tradesmen from the line: tailors, shoemakers, and anyone whose professional expertise might serve the needs of the conquering army. The eight hundred men remaining, who were of no use to the Nazis, including the elderly, the frail and exhausted, were marched the thirty kilometers to the barracks at the Zambrow forced labor camp in Eastern Prussia, where they awaited their transport to Auschwitz-Birkenau. Along the way, the Germans began Operation Harvest Festival — shooting, mass murder of the weak and ill who fell to their deaths. Fellow residents of our town met their end on that march: Berel Weinberg, Moshe Groshko, Girshon Friedman, Dov Avraham Balamot and his son. Moshe Hirsch Kivako suffered a nervous breakdown and threw himself into a well where he drowned. The others — those who survived the march — were taken to the Zambrow concentration camp, where they were sorted into who would be sent to Stahlbach and who to the Lomza detention camp. The beer merchant, Yodel Zilbrfing, who was caught when he went to buy beer from the distillery in the village of Vyshkov, was killed by gunfire.

Two fabric shops opened up in the ghetto. One was in the home of Isaac Kropinsky and the other was at the home of the shoemaker, Ephraim Stern. Craftspeople such as shoemakers, tailors, furriers, carpenters, metalworkers and others received a work permit and they were able to go to the nearby villages to work in exchange for food. Those who worked in the villages were able to buy goods from the Polish peasants and to bring them back for their families. A beloved friend of our family,

Leibl Frost spoke of how on his seven-kilometer walk to work, with his sack over his shoulder, he conducted flax trades. His mother would heat up the flax that he bought from the peasants for warmth. Then she squeezed out the water until it produced a low-grade oil. His family would then sell this oil to the locals in exchange for flour, wheat or other grains. The Frost family home had an oven, and when there was flour, they would bake bread. Occasionally Leibl could pick cabbage or beets from the fields without the Germans noticing. Sometimes Leibl didn't return home from work at all, because conditions within the ghetto were so grim that he preferred to remain outside its walls. On account of the crowding, he often slept outside, under the open sky.

Mass famine swept the ghetto. The shortage of food, the poverty, the physical torment, the overcrowding — the ghetto as a whole was suffering and starvation claimed victims daily. The Nazis gave them no more than starvation rations. The Jews who weren't working had to make do with just 184 calories a day, while Poles who lived outside the ghetto were given food with a caloric value of 699 and the Nazis fed themselves on at least 2,600 calories per day. The food was of poor quality: the flour was full of worms; the potatoes and other vegetables were rotten. There were Jews who stole, snatching food from one another. There was humiliation and loss of dignity. The uncertainty as to where the next meal would come from was a perpetual threat. The elderly, the poor, and the solitary lived in a firehall and were supported financially by the Judenrat's treasury. Some of them were "adopted" by the ghetto families. Children would stray like sheep in the farmers' fields. When asked where their parents were, they would point toward the forest. "There," they said. They begged for alms and died in the streets. Existential need forced them to flee the ghetto, which itself was a life-threatening endeavor. Children that were small, thin and flexible managed to sneak through the barbed-wire fence and sneak in some food from the town's Christian quarter. Sometimes youth who worked outside the ghetto brought a stock of rotten tree roots to maintain the fires in the fireplaces.

The ghetto became a place of impurity and death. The conditions created life-threatening sanitation and hygiene problems for ghetto residents. There was a shortage of water, of soap. Contamination led to disease. Tuberculosis, typhus and dysentery spread throughout the ghetto. Medical treatment was extremely poor. The odors of urine and feces did not dissipate but stuck to people's clothes and their destroyed bodies. Dr. Golda risked her life helping and caring for the sick, but the stock of medicines was meager, and she only managed to save a few people. Terrible crowding took over the ghetto that was built around just a few streets. People who were exhausted and unable to find a place to stay were thrown into the streets or gathered at entrances to homes. Dead bodies and trash were piled in the streets. Jews who had lost their humanity roamed hungry, shaking from the cold in their worn-out clothes. Anyone who fell ill lost his permit to work which was the only thing way one could hope to make a living. If they were put to work, it bought them a spark of hope, a signal that even though their lives were so bitter, they could continue on in spite of everything. There was no way of heating the houses. The ghetto residents piled doors, doorposts, broken shingles and any flammable material that remained from the ruined houses and set fire to them for heating. They were all pursued by fate, struck by grief, like silent, wandering shadows, knowing some would live and others would die. The nights left them without light, without hope, without knowing what would become of them. Sometimes they forgot that they were still people. They thought of themselves as the dead, shadowy entities disappearing into the void. The exhausting daily struggle was accompanied by despair and suicide.

A black market of smuggled food opened up in the ghetto. It was run by Jews who worked outside and thus managed to bring food in under the noses of the Nazis and their Polish collaborators. There was profiteering: children of 7 to 13 who were small enough to pass through tunnels and cracks in ruined buildings, would sneak in and steal food from the dwindling market stalls. For women it was easier to slip outside the ghetto, as their Jewishness was easier to disguise. Jews stole food from one another. Beggars asking for alms crowded the streets. The ghetto gradually became a mass prison with its prisoners slowly dying while doing hard work in harsh and inhumane conditions. This was the Nazis' starvation policy — to get rid of the Jews without wasting a single bullet from their stores of ammunition.

Living conditions in the ghetto got worse from day to day and the Jews lived in constant fear for their lives. To make it even more difficult, and to strike more fiercely at their fate, the Nazis resorted to cruel, collective punishment for any act of protest or refusal to obey an order. They even did the impossible — they issued an order requiring the Jews to pay fines of twenty thousand zlotys to the German authorities. This was meant as revenge for the German commissar occupying an apartment in a Christian neighborhood where no Jews had ever lived. The apartment had bedbugs which infuriated him. The Jews fought stubbornly for their survival; to hold onto life and hope for a better future were more important than anything.

There were no means of communication in the ghetto and its residents did not know what was happening elsewhere in the war. Later on, one of the Gentiles got a radio receiver and would take it out to the balcony of his home so that the ghetto residents could hear the news concerning the war. In this way they were able to follow the progress of the German army toward Moscow. Later, my grandfather — my mother's father, Shmuel Izak, would buy the Yiddish newspaper *De Werte* (Yiddish: *The Word*). The local Jewish bonds organization also had its own newspaper — the *Platz Zeitung* (Yiddish: Local Newspaper). Other Jewish newspapers were also occasionally smuggled into the ghetto. Every evening, at the end of the workday, Jews gathered together to read it, so they could know what was happening in the battlefields of the Russian-German war.

Jews that fled Warsaw and its surroundings to our

town reported the liquidation of ghettos all over Poland. In the Wysokie ghetto, the fear and feeling of disaster grew. On the night of November 1, 1942, the ghetto was surrounded by Germans and policemen, and from then on began the hardest days for European Jewry.

CHAPTER 5

Ghetto Liquidation and the Mazura Forest

In October, a black cloud was already hovering over the ghetto. On the night of November 1st, 1942, the evening before Yom Kippur, Dad heard the roar of motorcycles ridden by SS soldiers surrounding the ghetto. He also saw members of the Polish gendarmerie scouring the fences that encircled it, reinforcing its gates so that it was entirely secured without any way to escape. "That morning, to our horror, we saw that the Nazis had brought a fleet of some 600 horses which stood outside the ghetto walls, harnessed to their wagons. Fear spread quickly. We knew that something disastrous was about to happen."

That evening, Lazer-Yosef arrived with his cart of food from the Judenrat and confirmed the rumors. When he asked the Nazis why the horses and wagons were waiting outside the ghetto gates, the SS and the gendarmerie replied that the "transport fleet" was carrying saplings intended to be planted in the Mazura forest, which was thick with foliage as it was. "Their reply was suspicious. I realized that they were planning to kill every last one of us in the ghetto," Dad said.

It was a sleepless night for the residents of the ghetto. They still did not know what awaited them, but everyone feared what was to come. Despairing, they crowded together in their dilapidated houses, sitting or lying huddled together, trying to keep warm and take comfort in their loved ones. Mothers held their children tightly in their laps, fearing that they would no longer be able to protect them. Women packed the meager belongings that remained and dressed their children in many layers to protect them from the brutal frost outside. The children's faces were wan, their hands as skinny as twigs. Only their eyes burned: the deep, black eyes of Jewish children. They too were afraid. They didn't speak or cry or complain but understood everything. They knew that now they would be taken "there," to the places from which nobody ever returned. They did not understand why this was happening; they did not even know what crime it was that they were being punished for. They felt the breath of death on their small, exposed throats. But despite their despair, they were already accustomed to suffering.

"I don't have the words to express what we felt when we knew that we were going to be expelled from the ghetto," Dad said.

Sure enough, during the day of November 2nd, 1942, in order to realize the threat that hung over them, Nazi Schwartz appeared. The ghetto camp commander, armed with a rifle to make sure that no one escaped, gave orders to the Polish representatives of the town.

Rioting spread like wildfire threatening to annihilate everything. Jews tried to escape between the fences and gates, running around the barbed-wire fence, each trying to break out and run for his life. But those attempts were immediately thwarted by the police shooting. With violent roars and bamboo sticks, they flogged their victims. Even still, some hundred and fifty of the ghetto's inhabitants managed to escape through the barbed wire. Dad, who had scraped his thin body on the sharp fence was among those who managed to escape. He walked through the woods hoping to find members of his family, but the chaos was so terrible that he did not find any of them. Toward evening he met his father, Grandpa Fischel Yeruham, and together they made their way through the woods and fields hoping to happen upon anyone from their beloved family on their way.

"I can still hear the shouts of 'Mama! Papa!'" my father told me; his blue eyes black with uncontrollable anger. "In my mind's eye I still see those families that were separated, spread in every direction, children lost their parents, they became orphans, went hungry, tried to flee for their lives. I saw heartbreaking scenes. My ears still listen for the crying voices of abandoned children searching for their parents and the parents looking everywhere for their children. Those cries will echo in my memory forever.

"My friend David Gobolsky and I couldn't bear the pain," my father went on. "Everywhere was chaos. But a Gentile who knew me well, we used to do business together, gave us four loaves of bread. We returned to the spot where the desperate children had gathered, sliced and divided up the bread between them," Dad concluded the horrors that remain with him ever since.

As they were being forced out, the Jews were fleeing their homes, scared for their lives. The men raised their hands in surrender, but the Nazis closed around them and fired at them with machine guns.

"Run, run!" Inhuman screams were heard. Trained Nazi soldiers slaughtered the men. "Any man found in his home will be killed like a dog," they threatened.

Around two thousand men were already being whipped and lined up in the ghetto plaza. Many were laid out on the ground. The wounded howled, rolling and bleeding in the dirt all night.

In the morning, SS barbers violently cut the hair and beards of the Jewish men. There were no mirrors to reflect their new appearance, but their eyes flared with hatred of the Germans. Pleading for their lives, the Jews looked like chickens before the slaughter, like a chicken whose beard had been plucked, ripped from the skin of his face.

"Everyone outside!" The shouts were heard as a barrage of gunfire was released into the ghetto crowd. Ghetto inhabitants had to pass through two lines of Germans holding whips, being beaten from both sides with murderous lashes. Heads were split, eyes blinded and ribs broken. The Germans set fire to small prayer shawls, traditional frock coats (*bekishes*), wigs and beards. Within a few hours, the men were shaven, thin, and shaking, looking as though they had come from some other world.

The Germans set fire to the main ghetto square. Pillars of smoke and flames billowed. The sky was gray and heavy. The people looked to the sky, seeking mercy from God, but He was nowhere to be found.

Around two thousand Jews now stood outside the ghetto, surrounded and shackled by the enemy. German soldiers wearing helmets and carrying machine guns infiltrated the ghetto streets with cries and roars of "Out, out! (*Heraus, Heraus!*)." Wailing, tortured, humiliated, wounded and bloodied, unable to take any of their belongings, the Jews were expelled from their homes.

Amid the turmoil that ensued, using iron rods, knives, and every sharp tool they could find, Jewish men managed to tear rents into the barbed-wire fence. That was how they rescued their wives and mothers. Around one hundred thin children with their flexible bodies, also found cracks in the barbed-wire fence and escaped. In the din and chaos, Dad and Grandpa lost the rest of their family and didn't know if they had managed to escape or if they were even alive. Nobody knew who had fled and who had been captured by the Nazis. No one knew what had become of his loved ones.

In the midst of the turmoil, the Nazis loaded the wagons with the Jews and drove them about 30 kilometers to the Zambrow camp. The Nazis, aided by the Polish collaborators, gathered those too weak to make the walk into the market square. There they were shot down by a machine gun, one after the other, into the pit that was dug for them.

That was how the ghetto was liquidated in Wysokie Mazowickie. Beyond the ghetto fence and on the roadside, Gentiles stood and cheered, watching the tragic sight with satisfaction.

The Gentiles were already planning to rob the Jewish homes and take them over. The Poles laughed and were glad to see the deportees facing their execution. "They'll make soap out of you," they shouted. And indeed, that very day, just several days before Yom Kippur, the Christians living outside the ghetto were transferred into the houses of the displaced Jews.

Ghetto residents who were caught trying to escape were put on the waiting wagons. Their arms were tied to one another and their legs, bound with wire cables, were tied to the sides of the wagons. Armed guards stood at the ready between each two wagons. When there was no space left, the remaining captives trudged along after them on foot. They were brought to the concentration camp in the town of Zambrow which served the Nazis as a transit camp before Auschwitz-Birkenau. That was how the magnificent Jewish community that had flourished in the Diaspora for some three centuries met its end. This was but another chapter in the Nazi approach to the Jewish problem.

After the liquidation, only the dog that roamed the streets of the empty encampment remained. A rattle passed through the bones of the orphaned, creature, the guard of the ruined town. He too was starving and too hungry to go on whining.

Meanwhile, as their parents were being deported from the ghetto, a group of Jewish youths, heavily guarded, were paving and repairing the roads that had been damaged by the Luftwaffe bombing, and did not know what was going on in the ghetto. Suddenly the German foreman appeared at their workplace. Within several minutes, Germans armed with rifles joined him and ordered the fifty youth onto a truck. Nobody escaped, everyone did as they were told. The truck took them to the town of Rudka, where they were put in jail for six hours until they too were led onto wagons and joined the fleet of deportees in Zambrow.

In the morning, prior to deportation, Leibl and nine of his friends debated whether it would be safe to stay in their place of work. They worried that their absence would alarm the Nazis and rouse suspicion that their workers knew what was about to happen. Ultimately, despite many differing opinions, they decided to go to work anyway. On their way, a black cat crossed their path, which struck them as an omen of what was to come. Leibl recalled that just several days prior, the Nazis had sent many of Wysokie's Jews to the pits where they shot all of them. Leibl said to his friends, "Let's get back to the ghetto," but they resisted his suggestion. "Forget it, nothing is going to happen," they mocked him. "Don't say I didn't warn you," he said.

The ten friends went to work on the roads as planned. When they arrived, the Nazi Erik was a step ahead of them and made sure that none of the workers were missing. Within a few seconds, all of the Jewish workers found themselves surrounded by Nazis pointing their rifles at them. Dozens of wagons were waiting for them. An SS soldier ordered them to get in. They did as they were told. Within an hour the group found itself imprisoned in Rudka, where they were joined by many other Jews brought from other work sites in nearby towns. The next day, Leibl and his friends were released and led onto the wagons — ten men to a group. Following every three wagons was a security wagon driven by the gendarmerie, armed with automatic rifles. Leibl and his friends already knew that many Jews from nearby towns had been killed on the way from Rudka to Zambrow and that they too were now being led to the slaughter. The prisoners decided unanimously, "We will not go to the pits no matter what. The first chance we get, we'll jump from the wagon." Leibl Frost and his dear friend Roman were sitting in the wagon with eight other prisoners. Leibl's arm was tied to Roman's arm, and their legs were also tied together. All of them were tied with cables to the boards of the wagon. The two looked at one another and decided to run. They began to gnaw on the ropes with their teeth, trying to break free. They chewed as hard as they could, wetting the ropes with their spit, and finally managed to tear through them. When their arms were free, they untied their friends one by one and together they released the wires that bound them to the wagon. Once they had removed the cables, they had just to wait for the right moment to jump off. The Gentile wagon driver said, "So you know, you're being taken to the pits."

When the wagon passed by the town of Kuski, which was right beside a dense forest, a young couple that was roaming the forest approached them and asked the wagon driver about the horse that was pulling the wagon. While the Nazi guard was getting rid of the wandering couple, he turned a blind eye and Leibl and Roman fled to the town. The Nazis shot after them. But the two friends were young and quick-footed and managed to escape the enemy bullets. At this opportunity, others from the town also fled: Ephraim Mazor, Isak Sokal and Yakov Tikchinsky. The escapees hid in the forest the whole night. Members of the Polish guard that kept watch on the entrances to the forest, opened fire but missed the fugitives who ran in zigzags through the thick brush. With daylight, they decided to make their way to the town of Galicia.

Winter temperatures dropped daily, and everyone feared the snows that would overrun the forest. The first snow of winter came one night and covered everything. At dawn, on their way through the forest, Leibl and Roman noticed two figures through the trees, approaching them. Their hearts nearly stopped with fear of being caught by the Polish militia whose blue berets were visible from every angle, as they scoured the forest. As Leibl Frost and Roman hid from them, so did the others. But as they neared one another they discovered, to their great relief, that the suspicious figures were none other than their dear friends Avi Pesach Segal and his father — my grandfather Fischel Yeruham Segal. The four men embraced one another and cried on each other's shoulders. Leibl had a "treasure with him, a fresh loaf of rye bread, warm and crunchy with caraway seeds inside, that he had received as a gift from the Gentile Sosonovsky who had worked for his family's flour mill in the past. He had pressed the bread into Leibl's hands when he was the last to return to the cart before leaving. My grandfather refused to eat Leibl's bread. "You were fortunate to receive this loaf of bread. Save it for yourself and it will carry you a long way," he said. But Leibl insisted, saying, "In these times, with our lives hanging by a thread, we cannot miss any opportunity. We must make the most of what we have left." The four men sat down on the freezing ground. Leibl set down the warm bread, divided it into portions and distributed it among them. As they took bites from it, their tears moistened the bread.

Leibl and Roman parted ways from my father and grandfather. The four continued to walk in the Mazura Forest, hoping to find other surviving members of their families. There were already some hundred and fifty Jews hiding in the forest who had escaped the liquidation of the Wysokie ghetto on November 2, 1942. There my father and grandfather found my grandmother, Sarah Segal, hiding in a dugout with other Jews from the town. Her only daughter, my aunt Rivka, was not with her and my uncle Shia was absent too. Nobody knew if they were still alive. To hide from the Nazis, Grandpa dug a hole and covered it with branches and grasses, then crept inside together with my grandmother. Dad helped his parents hide. Then they dug pits for the others in which they and their families hid. That was how Wysokie's Jews made their homes in the forest. At night they ventured out to the villages to get some food and then, usually still hungry, they returned to their hiding places once more.

Before dawn on November 14, Leibl's younger brother Mordechai showed up to the Mazura forest, bringing a bit of food that his parents had sent from their hiding place at the home of a Gentile in Kolonia. When Leibl found out about his parents' hiding place, he crawled out of the trench where he had been hiding and made his way to them. But when he got to their hiding place the place was already empty. Leibl left Mordechai in the shelter where his parents had previously been, and which was now a meeting place for Jews who had managed to escape. As Leibl comforted his younger brother, he suddenly saw before him the barrel of a machine gun squeeze into the shelter.

"Out! Everybody out!" The Nazi Erik bellowed. His evil was known to everyone, which was why the Jews called him "the Basher," the killer with a stick. "The Basher is coming, the Basher is back, the Basher is on his way…" This was how the Jews expressed the horror all around them. The Nazi pulled everyone out from the bunker in which they were hiding. Then he began to fire in every direction. People dropped like flies, but the bullets missed Leibl and his younger brother. A hundred people survived the wild shooting. The SS lined up the survivors in rows. The entire Mazura Forest was surrounded by Germans and Polish collaborators.

Leibl saw the Basher approach the bush where my grandfather and grandmother were hiding. The Nazi told my grandfather to open his mouth. As he forced his gun into my grandfather's mouth, he shouted, "Where did you hide the gold, Segal? Where did you hide the money that you made in the flour mill?" My grandfather gripped the man's arm, trying to pull the gun from his mouth, but the evil hacker shot his gun straight into his throat. My grandfather died on the spot, parts of his brain scattering and falling on the body of my grandmother

Sarah who was huddled in his arms. My grandmother was shot in her leg but managed to get away. Nobody ever found out for certain what became of her. We believe that she was transported along with other people from our town to Auschwitz-Birkenau where she would have perished in the gas chambers.

Then the Basher approached Hersch-Yitzhak Trastovacz and shot him through the mouth too. Hersch-Yitzhak crumpled over, dead on the spot. When he finished, the Basher ordered the hundred Jews who had survived the massacre to get in line and then killed them with an automatic rifle. The forest floor was colored red with Jewish blood. Those Jews that weren't wounded or hurt, among them my uncle Shia and my aunt Rivka, were taken by the Nazis to Wysokie, where they were put into a horse stable which served as a prison. They spent the night there, in terrible crowding with around two hundred other prisoners, with air as hot and stuffy as in a furnace. When the Nazis opened the stables in the morning, there were already dozens of suffocated Jews lying on the ground. An officer of the Polish gendarmerie appeared holding a gun, and opened with shouts and insults, "Killers like you, I know you're all partisans, you are active in the woods and want to kill us, but we're not like that, we'll send you to the labor camp." It was not long before all the survivors of the forest massacre, including my aunt Rivka and Uncle Shia, were taken by transport to Auschwitz-Birkenau.

On the afternoon of November 14th, 1942, while the Nazis were slaughtering his family, my father, terrified, had hidden in a farther trench with some of his friends, listening to the sound of shots at close range and dogs barking. Shouts of *"Heraus!"* tore through the silence of the forest. Dad stuck his head out of the trench he was in and saw, to his astonishment, Polish and German gendarmerie wildly pulling those Jews who had survived thus far out of the ground. Gendarmes lined them up in rows. Like a cannibal, his eyes burning black and his automatic rifle in his hands, the Basher commanded, "Bring me the son of the Hertz family out of the trench, or else I'll shoot him plus an additional twenty Jews." Then without waiting, he opened fire. David Gozovsky, Yadek Aharon Hertz, David Becker and dozens of other Jews were killed on the spot. As SS officers were brutally slaying Jews at close range, the terrible Nazi pulled his gun and aimed it right at Dad's temple and roared an order for him to get out of the line. The roar of the Jewish crowd from the other rows drew the Nazi's attention for a split second and he looked back. Dad did not miss a moment. In the chaos he seized the opportunity and took off, fleeing into the thick of the forest with the Basher in hot pursuit, shooting live fire after him, determined to catch him, alive or dead. The bullets whistled over Dad's head, but he ran without thinking where he was going. He seemed to pass through walls, broken tree branches and the brush which covered them like a curtain. Thanks to his military training (he had been a soldier in the Polish army), Dad knew he had to run in zigzags between the trees, which was how he managed to dodge the bullets and survive.

Running, Dad reached the edge of the forest. There, a green meadow opened up before him; he would not be hidden by the low bushes. From his knowledge of the forest, he knew that a canal passed close by, a tributary of the Bug river that crossed their town, separating the Jewish neighborhood from the Christian-Catholic neighborhood. Dad rolled into the canal. Its freezing waters hurt his bones which were weak from the frantic run, but Erik didn't see him. Tired and giving up on capturing Dad, the Nazi returned to the spot where the bodies of Jews lay bleeding, dying or dead. When the Nazis finally left, Dad returned to the location of the massacre that had taken place while he was running, fleeing for his life and hiding from that wicked Nazi.

Once again separated from his family, Dad continued to wander alone in the woods. For a long time he could not decide whether to continue hiding or return to the town. Danger was everywhere. The winter froze his bones, but his spirit stayed strong. His insight told him that any decision he made might bring about his death, so he gambled and decided to return to Wysokie, to the spacious family home, now inhabited by Polish and Nazi invaders.

To his great surprise, Dad found his brother Haim in the yard. Haim had hidden in the home of a Polish acquaintance, Danek Kirshnovsky, whose family was one of those now living in our family's home. Dad also met the Gentile Watzek Bialitsky there, a mechanic who had worked in their flour mill before the war. Watzek arranged a shelter for him and Haim and they moved to hide in the warehouse for animal feed behind the house. None of this happened before the brothers paid a small fortune to the two Gentiles. Kirshnovsky took care of them secretly and with great dedication and would take the great risk of bringing them food, all without the knowledge of his family and other invading families on our estate. Dad worried that if their identities were learned by his wife or children, they would surely hand them over to the Nazis.

Once, on December 13, 1942, while they were in their hiding place, they had a very close brush with death. A Polish peasant who had worked in the family's flour mill before the war, gave up their hiding place to the Nazis. The noble-minded Kirshnovsky was "granted" a visit by the German gendarmerie. They beat him badly and demanded that he hand over the refugees in his care. He vehemently denied ever having hidden Jews, but the Nazis did not believe him and began to search everywhere for them. They turned over every item in the home, broke the floors, knocked on the walls, dug in the yard, and still the gentleman stood by his decision to protect them. Fortunately, both for them and their savior, the Nazis did not manage to find the shelter. Frustrated and furious, they left. It was clear, however, that from then on, the Nazis would not let Kirshnovsky be. Now there was nothing left but for the escapees to leave, to escape once again and take shelter among the fields and trees of the forest. The next day, December 14, Dad and Uncle Haim left.

A new episode of wandering and hiding began. Dad

and Haim hid in silos and barns, suffering from cold and hunger. The fear of being discovered by the Germans or their Polish collaborators gnawed at them constantly. They had to act quickly. They couldn't wait around for a miracle, and anyway they had to leave the forest every once in a while to look for bread. The brothers knew all of the farmers in the surrounding area who, before the war, would come to their flour mill to grind their crops at harvest time, but rarely did these Gentiles show any willingness to help, either out of fear of the Nazis or simple anti-Semitism. Only rarely did they manage to appease their hunger. And so Dad and Haim survived in the forest, hungry, freezing and exhausted, for about five months — until March of 1943.

In the fields and between the dense brush of the forest Dad and Haim met Jews from their town who, like them, were also wandering the woods hungry and exhausted, trying to find shelter and a little bread. Sometimes whole days passed before they had anything to eat. The forest was full of Polish Gentiles, prisoners of war and Russian war deserters who had fled the Red Army. They abused the Jews, looted and robbed them. Any one of them could end their lives. In order to fight the abuse, Dad and Haim used to put a boot on one foot and a shoe on the other. They hid the other boot, hoping that a single boot would not be worth stealing. In order to survive and fight against the plunderers, the Jews organized themselves into large groups and fought with branches that they had torn from trees. This, despite the danger that such a gathering would make it easier for the Nazi killers to notice them.

From their longstanding acquaintances with their drunken Gentile neighbors, Dad and Haim knew how to work them in order to survive the constant battle against starvation. Occasionally the brothers would knock on the door of one of the peasants and ask to buy vodka from him. The Gentiles, most of whom knew our family, would then invite them into their home. From the small amount of money that they had managed to sneak into the forest, Dad and Haim paid for the vodka. On these occasions, the Gentiles, so as not to drink on an empty stomach, would lay out the table with appetizers, a little bread, some pork fat and salted fish. They would grow cheerful and unrestrained when they drank, and in their drunken state, the peasants usually invited the hungry Jews to eat and drink with them. They even occasionally sent them off with some leftover food.

One dark night, when the brothers could no longer

stand the cold and the hunger, they suddenly saw two lights flashing in the distance. Cautiously, they advanced toward them and arrived at two huts of Polish peasants. They gambled on one of the huts and knocked on the door. As an excuse, they asked the man of the house to use his fire as a light for their cigarettes. It was the home of Yanovitz. The Gentile invited them inside. They feared that he had set a trap for them, but as they observed his household, the brothers felt that they were not in any danger. They gave the Gentile a little money and asked him to go to the village and buy vodka for them. The villager sent his son to the nearby village of Ryki to buy the vodka. Haim remained in the hut, while Dad went outside to keep watch in case of any oncoming danger, lest the son take the money for himself and instead of returning with the vodka, bringing the Polish militia back with him. Luckily for them, Yanovitz junior did not cheat them; he returned with the requested bottle. Dad opened it and said to the members of the household, "Now, our dear hosts, let us drink to your health!" He filled the glasses and the farmer brought refreshments. They thanked the generous Gentile and his family and gave them their blessings. Another time, knocking on other gentile doors, the brothers repeated the "festivities" of vodka, pork fat and salted fish.

At the end of March 1943, Dad and Haim went to visit Kirshnovsky who had also worked at their flour mill before the war. They told him that somewhere in the woods they had buried a cache, and if he would be willing to hide them, they would reward him handsomely. They came to an agreement regarding the amount of zloty he would receive if he saved their lives. Kirshnovsky built a shelter for them in the field, beside the silo wall, inside piles of straw. The entrance was through the cowshed. Tobacco leaves grew above the shelter, hiding the place. The farmer and his family, who also knew about the hiding place, would bring the refugees coffee with a little milk, hot soup and some bread.

Then the Nazis discovered a nearby hideout of Jews being sheltered by Polish families and executed them all, so Kirshnovsky was afraid to go on hiding them. But when Dad and Haim promised him that the war would end within three months, the merciful Gentile allowed them to remain under his protection. When the war refused to end, the Gentile's patience grew thin and, for lack of another option, asked them to leave. They returned to the forests and the fields where spring had already begun to bloom, so the brothers managed to survive another six months. In the meantime, rumors had reached them that some 2,000 Jews that had been deported from the ghetto in November of 1942 were taken to a transit and extermination camp, and between the 11th and the 17th of January, 1943, they were taken to Auschwitz where most of them were murdered. Among them were Grandma Sarah, my aunt Rivka and my uncle Shia.

Then in the summer of 1944, rumors from the front began to arrive that the German army was being defeated in battle and the Red Army was advancing toward our town. So Dad and Haim returned to Kirshnovsky, who was willing to take them under his protection once more. The brothers remained in his shelter until August 1944, when the town was liberated by the Russians. Dad and Haim returned to their Wysokie. At the end of 1944, when the war ended in our region, of the approximately 2,500 Jews who had lived in the town, only 30 remained. When Auschwitz-Birkenau was liberated, hundreds of Jews from our town, who had been imprisoned there, were transported on foot — the death march from Auschwitz to the Mauthausen camp in Austria. Most of them died on the way or were murdered at their destination.

Gradually, the survivors of the ghettos, the extermination camps, Auschwitz, Mauthausen, Treblinka and others began to return to Wysokie. There, the remaining Jews united. Among the survivors, Dad and Haim met my mom, Rivka Yelin, along with the four surviving members of her family of nine: my grandfather, Shmuel Izak, and his children, Mom, Hezkel, Basha and Dverka.

That was how my parents met and in May 1945, in the ruined city, they held their wedding canopy. I was born in the town of Wysokie Mazowickie on February 14, 1946. The Russians, who had defeated the Germans, now annexed our town and established a Communist regime that did not allow the Jewish survivors to leave the borders of Poland. All over Poland, most families of survivors left their ruined hometowns where they always lived and moved to the big cities such as Poznan, Lodz and Wroclaw. Others went to Bergen-Belsen and other DP camps. In the summer of 1946, half a year after my birth, we too moved to live in Wroclaw to await the permit that would grant us the right to leave Poland. There, on June 16, 1948, my sister Rachela was born.

The Gentiles who had hidden my relatives often came to visit us in Wroclaw. Later, I heard from a relative that Dad had handed over all of his family's property in Wysokie including their flour mill, to the kind-hearted Gentile Bialitsky.

Only in May of 1950 did Poland's communist gates open and we received our permit — we were finally allowed to leave Poland. Mom and Dad decided to move to Israel while most of our surviving relatives made new lives for themselves in the United States, Australia and other Diaspora communities around the world. On the dilapidated Greek ship *Anatolia*, we made our journey to the two-year-old State of Israel.

Dad lost his father, his mother, his brother Shia and his sister Rivka in the war. His eldest brother Meishke was kidnapped by the Russians at the beginning of the war and exiled to Kazakhstan in Siberia. He lived there under the Communist regime, unable to see his brothers again. Mom, on the other hand, lost her mother Rachel, her brother Arieh, and her sisters Chirla and Chaya. Her father, Shmuel Izak, her brother Hezkel, and her sisters Dverka and Basha survived and immigrated, some to the US and others to Australia.

My mother was 17 years old when she was thrown into a small room in the ghetto where three other families also were crowded. She was 17 when her youth was taken from her. One evening Dad tried to summarize what happened to him and his family during those six years. He turned to me gently and said, "Your mother was a young woman when the Nazis invaded Wysokie and fenced off the Jewish quarter. But despite the six terrible years that she experienced, the light in her eyes did not go out and her appetite for life never faded. Determined not to give up all her power, she made her way through the rubble and began to rebuild her world. At age twenty-three, her cheekbones were still high, and her smile was accompanied by two charming dimples. Her slim, feminine figure was already mature, ready to build her family. At the end of the war, when my parents met again in the town, they were married.

"Your mother stood beside me in a white lace dress; the dowry that she had embroidered before the war. Tears of happiness sprung from the eyes of the guests. I wore my gray suit which was several sizes too big on my scrawny frame. It was a long time before I gained back the weight that I had dropped during those hungry years. While we were still struggling to manage with the loss and grief, you came into the world.

"When you were born, there were no doctors in the bombed-out hospital, and you were brought into our arms by some women from the town. After the years of leanness and suffering left your mother without milk in her breasts, we had to hire a Polish woman who had just birthed a son to feed you. But on her way to you, the Gentile would stop and nurse several other babies, and when she arrived at your hungry mouth she was totally emptied of her milk and nothing remained to sate your hunger. There were no milk substitutes back then and your wailing betrayed the deception. We had to fire her and do the impossible to feed you."

For almost three years my family wandered between the forests and villages. Occasionally, they were protected by Gentiles who had known them and their pre-war generosity, their polite and fair treatment of Gentiles. Many such Poles saved my family from certain death many times over.

Between 2006 to 2007, thanks to donations from an American-Jewish donor named Michael Traison, extensive restorations were carried out in the Wysokie Mazowickie cemetery which was renewed and remains in remembrance. Today, the town is inhabited by some 10,000 people of which not one is Jewish.

CHAPTER 6

Zambrow

Zambrow is a town in the Bialystok region in North Eastern Poland. Today it is home to around 23,000 people and serves as the capital city for the Zambrow county in the Lomza subdistrict. Jewish settlement in Zambrow began at the start of the 18th century. It was the birthplace of Rabbi Shlomo Goren, who served as the Military Rabbinate of the Israel Defense Forces.

Up until World War II, more than 3,500 Jews lived in the town, making up over half the population. As a result of their important influence on its daily life, Jewish character became a part of the city, but Jews' influence and commercial success led to increasing anti-Semitism.

In September of 1939, the Wehrmacht invaded Zambrow and stayed. In August 1941, the Zambrow ghetto was established. The ghetto was open to trade in agricultural produce that villagers brought and sold or traded, such that in the beginning, the Jews did not starve.

The ghetto was just two enclosed streets, surrounded by a sharp barbed-wire fence and bisected by a deep canal. There were some 2,000 Jews in the ghetto, but in time, the Nazis sent an additional 15,000 who had been deported from the surrounding towns of Wysokie Mazowickie, Lomza, Jablonka, Czyzew, Czarny Bor and others. They were forced to perform hard labor: paving roads, mining rocks, fixing sewers and the water supply network, loading and unloading at the Czarny Bor train station, building bridges, fixing and building new buildings in the big barracks that remained from the Russian regime.

One Thursday, September 4, 1941, the Nazis gathered Zambrow's Jews together in the nearby town of Rothke-Koski and murdered them en masse, killing some 1,000 of the city's Jews, including elderly people and pregnant women.

On November 2, 1942, the Nazis *liquidated* the Zambrow ghetto. In its place — in the barracks that the Russians had left behind — they built the infamous Zambrow concentration and extermination camp, which served as a transit station before being sent on to Auschwitz-Birkenau or Treblinka. The latter was around 30 kilometers away from Zambrow.

The camp was divided into seven barracks or "blocks". The crowding and living conditions were unbearable. Fourteen prisoners would be crammed onto a bunk built for six. The daily meal consisted of 150 grams of bread baked from bran and chestnut flour and half a liter of tasteless soup made from rotten potatoes. Only rarely were they able to receive a little hot water. When winter came, the snow began to fall and they found themselves in the army barracks, dressed in their tattered clothes, without mattresses or blankets. Around 100 people died each day.

Berel Sokal, who was imprisoned in Zambrow with 17 members of his family, could no longer stand to see the suffering of his wife, his parents and his children. He was fortunate to be employed, from four in the morning until seven in the evening, as an assistant in the camp kitchen. He carried water, cleaned and made sure that the kitchen was orderly. The kitchen manager — the Nazi Bloch — who was pleased with Berel's work, granted him additional food: three liters of soup plus radishes, beets and potatoes. Once in a while, when the guards weren't paying attention, he managed to steal a few extra potatoes. That was how Berel managed to feed his extended family and they survived the camp's hardships until the day of its liquidation. One day the Nazi kitchen workers asked to replace him, but Pesach Skovronek, the Jew in charge of the kitchen, insisted that Sokal remain in his position. Thanks to his support, Sokal stayed on, working in the kitchen until the camp was no more.

At its beginning, 17,500 Jews were imprisoned in Zambrow. Most of them were from Wysokie Mazowickie and the nearby towns. There the Nazis separated children from their parents. The cries were so loud that even the Nazis could not stand it and put the parents and children back together. When Jews arrived at the camp they did a special "ceremony." Inside a large hall, a cellar was dug out. The Nazis turned out the light in the hall and pushed all of the Jews into the dark pit. Dozens died right then and there.

For the most part, the Jews were not taken out to work, so it was left to the Nazis to keep them busy with endless abuse. One of their torture methods was to make the prisoners walk naked past a line of Germans who hit them with sticks and other implements. Another method was called "treks." These were daily walks in any weather. On these so-called treks, the Jews, including the elderly, the unwell, and children, were forced to walk barefoot and half naked for hours throughout the camp. Twice a day the prisoners were made to stand barefoot in the camp's yard in the fierce cold while the Nazis hit them with canes. Many, especially the sick and the weak, could not endure it. There was no limit to the Nazis' sadism and abuse. They threw hundreds of Jews into the pits that they had been forced to dig themselves and set them on fire. While two pits were burning, a third was used to hold the hot ash. Finally, the Nazis put the ashes of the dead in wheelbarrows and threw them into the big Vistula river.

With nothing to do, the Jews sat around, each man waiting for his turn to board a train whose destination was his demise. The Nazis would send groups of detainees to gather twigs in the woods from which they assembled broomsticks. Most of the time, the prisoners were kept busy sweeping the floors of the officers' living quarters. They were also made to dig the pits the intended purpose of which was unknown to them.

On December 31, 1942, ten prisoners from Wysokie, including Leibl Frost, Shalom Blumenkranz and his grandson Feivel-Moshe, were sent to do maintenance work outside the camp. At that time they still had a little money, so they bribed the German guards who turned a blind eye. The three of them went around the emptying stores and bought what was left of the bread. In total, they managed to buy somewhere between 15 and 20 kilograms of bread which they hid among the twigs they gathered in the woods. Back at the camp, they divided the bread between their hungry friends, but the Nazis discovered the smuggling. They ordered the group of prisoners who had bread to place it on the pile of twigs and walk away. They were interrogated *under torture* and the Nazis ordered them to turn in those who had bought the bread for them. When they refused, the Nazis ordered them to choose one prisoner who would accept the punishment for all of them. The friends did a lottery between them to determine which of them would be the unfortunate representative. Shalom Blumenkranz was the unlucky winner. He made his way over to the soldiers, as ordered. The Germans held a vicious, lusty, monstrous beating. Shalom returned swollen, bloody and sore. His friends compensated him for his suffering by giving him an even bigger piece of bread.

On the 10th of January 1943, the Nazis began to liquidate

the Zambrow camp and the Jews were sent to Auschwitz. But not before the Nazis made the prisoners dig large pits in the ground. To their question, "who are they being dug for?", the Nazis replied that they were meant to bury the garbage and dirt that had accumulated in the camp. Several days passed before it became clear that the pits were dug to bury 500 sick Jews who were in the camp's hospital, and indeed, they were shot into the pits. The Nazis also put the elderly and the children in the "hospital" block where the Nazis Bloch and Chandler, along with a Nazi doctor, poisoned the patients with "medicine" — a spoonful of poison that killed them instantly. At the same time, the Nazis carried out Aktions in the hospital, where 800 other hospitalized Jews, whose medical conditions were deteriorating, were eliminated.

All camp inmates were told that due to the terrible hygienic conditions prevailing in the camp, they would be driven some distance away each morning to work. On the morning of January 18, 1943, farmers' wagons were brought, people were loaded on, and taken to the nearby train station of Czyzew. With exemplary order and according to their towns of origin, Abraham-Berel Sokal, Leibl Frost, Yisrael Yelin, Ben Shilam, Yankel Delangitch, Bendt Pianco, Shlomo Tanenbaum, Haim

Kaviarat and Moshe Yossel Kassiar were taken by transport to Auschwitz.

The Jews that remained behind were gathered by the Nazis into the camp yard. That same dark, freezing night, the Nazis loaded those unable to walk onto the wagons. Exhausted, half naked, wrapped in rags, they were thrown like logs onto the wagons that had been confiscated from the local peasants. Some hundred and fifty people who were too weak to keep walking the Nazi's death march, froze to death. As he was riding, Berel Sokal suddenly saw four of his children, his wife and his elderly mother in a nearby cart. Suddenly it tipped over and they descended into the deep, soft snow. Berel tried to help them, but a blow to his head stopped him. Berel eventually managed to raise the cart and put his family members back on it. The cold was so intense that the children's tears froze. His mother said, "I wish I could just drown in the deep snow. If you had just left us buried underneath it, we would have been saved from having to board the train to our death." His children, his elderly mother and his wife continued on toward the train station.

From a bird's eye view, the Czyzew train station looked

like a mass of people, or a swarm of flies sitting on leather suitcases which contained the contents of their lives. While the train was coming to a stop at the station, the Nazis would strike its passengers with lashes, cramming them into the train cars. In an attempt to spare his family the blows, when he knew that there was no choice or chance to save them, Berel helped his family to board a train car as quickly as possible. In groups of 2,000 to 2,500 Jews, the detainees were transported, a hundred people in a train car intended for transporting cattle. Each passenger received a slice of bread as provisions for the journey. Then the Nazis locked the train cars and wrapped them with barbed wire. Without any of the passengers knowing their destination, the train sped off, its carriages crammed with its cargo of those sentenced to death. Many died of cold and were spared from what was to come. Just like that, without food or drink for three days straight, the Jewish victims were transported on the Czyzew-Auschwitz line.

On its way the train stopped at different stations. Thousands of Jews stood crammed together on the platforms, waiting for their fate. They warned the Zambrow passengers what was awaiting them, urging, "Run away! They're taking you to your death," but no one took their advice. Nobody believed it was possible. When they passed the death camp of Treblinka, the train stopped. Groups of Jews were taken out of the train cars and led in a single file line to the gates of the extermination camp — into the gaping maw of death. But even then, the Jews who remained behind on the train didn't know that they had just passed one of the largest Nazi killing factories. During these hours, news of the mass extermination had not yet reached them, nor any information about Auschwitz. So fierce was their belief and desire to live, that Leibl Frost and his friends refused to believe that they were destined for annihilation. Despite the crowding, cold and hunger on the train, even when they were on the verge of doom, they believed some miracle would save them. As the train continued hurtling along and they realized, to their relief, that they had not been let off at any of the stations, they grew even firmer in their belief that they were going to be safe.

At one station, before the train left, Polish guards stood on the platform and fired at those who managed to jump from the train and escape. Nonetheless, ten of the passengers from our town managed to escape, to squeeze through the barred windows and evade the guards' shooting. Among them were my uncle, my mother's brother, Leibl Frost, Hezkel Yelin, Ephraim Mazor, Itzik Walman, Haim, Lazer Yelin, Shmuel Susana, Hershel Weirovnik, and Herschel Zilberfenig, who fled to the dense forest. Other Jews who still had some money, also managed to escape and buy their lives and hiding places from the Gentiles.

Even Pesach Dalangwicz jumped and was saved from the shooting of the guards. All alone he survived the Holocaust, but at its end he had no strength left to go on living. Crushed and exhausted, he hung himself in our family's flour mill in Wysokie Mazowickie and died.

One evening friends and family gathered in our apartment's living room. The conversation revolved around the Zambrow extermination camp. Until that day, at age 12, I had not heard of the camp, and as I sat, huddled in an armchair in the corner of the room, I listened attentively to the adults' conversation. The things that were said that night prevented me from sleeping for a long time afterward. Hiding, I worried that my parents would discover me and send me to bed. The conversation was so intimate, piercing and painful that nobody noticed my presence or bothered to censor words unfit for my young ears.

Choked by tears, Berel said, "I was petrified. My heart wasn't big enough to contain all that pain. I do not know how I was brought to the Zambrow camp. Within twenty minutes, every member of my family passed by me to perish before my eyes. I stood naked in the entrance to the camp in the terrible cold. There they tattooed my left arm with the number 88966. When the Kapo (the Jew forced by the Nazis to help them torture and kill their peers) called me over to beat me, I no longer had any other name. '88966,' he called, and I had to bend over as he whipped me with a thick stick. Many Jews couldn't stand it; they left the line and walked to the group designated for death of their own initiative.

"There, in Zambrow, they cut the hair on my head and left me standing, frozen, in the camp yard, where the abuse was even worse than before. They sorted us again. They carved my serial number onto a tin plate, this time it was 120298."

His words shocked me. I wanted to plug my ears so as not to hear them. But I also wanted to listen and know everything. I felt that if all of my relatives and their friends had been through that inferno, it was my responsibility to identify with them in solidarity, to learn, to know and hear everything each one had to say about his bitter experience. And not only that but I felt obligated to pass on these stories of suffering.

On January 18, 1943, the Zambrow camp was liberated by the Red Army. The camp had operated for just forty-five days but had seen unimaginable tortures and killings. Hundreds of its inmates died in agony and those who survived were sent to Auschwitz or Treblinka, where almost everyone was murdered. Only five prisoners managed to escape their brothers' fate and save their lives.

CHAPTER 7

Death Breathing Down Their Necks

Auschwitz-Birkenau, June 1940 - May 1945

"Fifty years passed until I was able to talk about what happened to me there. All those years, the secret weighed on me; I couldn't even tell it to my wife and children — the family that I built in Israel after surviving that inferno that was Auschwitz-Birkenau. 'We don't talk about that *here*,' I used to dodge their pleas to know. I didn't have the strength to handle it, to return to that place and share the tragedy that I experienced. Maybe I was also ashamed of my own actions, and of being criticized. I was worried that they would not understand my predicament. I refused to open so much as a crack into that despicable world of Auschwitz. I wanted to numb every emotion, numb the pain. It was only when my daughter returned home from an educational trip to Auschwitz-Birkenau, upset by what she saw, that I changed my mind. My trauma, remorse, horror and shame rose up, burst out and became common knowledge."

When he told his story from the Holocaust, Leibl Frost revisited the experience as though it were yesterday: the torments and the horrors of that bloody, hateful, unparalleled period in human history. In his mind's eye he saw the murderers, bloodthirsty, shooting at helpless women and children as they writhed in agony, the blood that flowed from the dying bodies, the gas chambers and the heaps of corpses. He recalled the thick black smoke that rose up out of the Auschwitz-Birkenau crematorium. His fears returned to him. There was one line that continued to bother him, "For now I'm still alive, but soon it will be my turn for my body to go up in flames and smoke, be lifted and swallowed up into the clouds and fill the sky."

Leibl was one of some 2,000 Jewish prisoners who had arrived on the transport from the town of Wysokie Mazowickie and its surrounding villages. The train cars were crammed with sweaty bodies curled up, sticking to one another, hearts racing. Fear of what came next paralyzed them. The air was dense, everyone gasping for breath, trying to stretch his nose toward some window for a little air. A thin, lifeless, old man leaned his head on Leibl's shoulder. The man held a piece of bread in his hand that swung with the train as it sped along its tracks. The man was dying. Leibl looked hungrily at the piece of bread in the man's hand. He waited for him to die so that he could take it from him without stealing from his hungry, dying belly. "Where is the train headed?" Leibl asked himself. "What will happen to those who remained behind? At home? In the ghetto? Or at the Zambrow camp?" But nobody knew the answers to his questions. They were insignificant in the world of chaos, fear, terror, confusion and distress that was Auschwitz.

After three days of traveling — on January 20, 1943 — the train came to a stop with a cloud of smoke. The carriage doors were unlocked and opened wide. They heard shouting: *"Heraus! Heraus!* (Out! Out!), leave the suitcases! Set down all the belongings you brought! Quietly!" The shouts filled the space of the station. Arms crossed and blinded by the light; the Jews got off the train. With batons, the uniformed SS men, wearing black visored caps with the skull symbol on it, pushed them straight to the 'Jewish terminal' of the Auschwitz I concentration camp. So began the torture that was to last around three years.

At the entrance, above the camp's gate, the following sign greeted its entrants: "*Arbeit macht frei*" or "work will set you free". That and the network of railroad tracks that transported those being taken to their deaths would be considered symbols of the Nazi's crimes.

Auschwitz I

Before World War II, Auschwitz, or Oswiecim in Polish, was a town in upper Silesia, some 50 kilometers from Krakow on the banks of the Sola River — a tributary of the Upper Vistula River. The camp was previously an abandoned Polish military base. In the 19th century, the city served as a base for the Austro-Hungarian Empire's cavalry. In 1940, the Third Reich annexed the barracks and designated it as a camp for enemies of the regime — Polish elites, socialists, Communists and Russian prisoners. They called it "Auschwitz 1". In 1941 the Nazis turned it into the killing factory the likes of which had never been seen before or has since. The camp was rectangular in shape and spanned 60 square kilometers.

It was surrounded by a double electric fence, four meters tall, that encircled the entire grounds. The site included 29 wooden buildings, two stories high and arranged in three rows of "Blocks". There were moats and guard towers which could see hundreds of meters — even kilometers — in all directions. At each tower, armed SS guards were stationed with angry dogs (the letters "SS" stood for the German word *schutztaffel*, "protection squadron"). Before Hitler had been appointed German chancellor, these brigades served as his personal security. But after he rose to power and was made Fuhrer, he assigned these divisions to carry out the work of execution. The SS organization numbered 250 thousand men, brainwashed with Nazi ideology, which became the Nazi defense and military intelligence corps. Later this unit became an entire guard division. Since Auschwitz had originally been built as a Polish army base, each building now used as a block had a number and the streets bore the names of cherries and flowers. The Nazis crammed their victims — the detainees constantly arriving on transports from all across Europe — into these buildings.

Auschwitz I was the first and largest concentration

camp out of the 2,000 different camps that the Nazis established and that operated for the longest time (from June 1940 until May 1945). At first, the camp served the Nazis as an administrative center for their extermination system. Apart from carrying out death sentences, the camp was meant to supply a workforce of Jews, Soviets and Poles, to build a future German industrial city and a network of train stations to transport the victims to their destruction at its various facilities. There, the Nazis carried out their preliminary experiments on Polish and Soviet prisoners, whom the Wehrmacht had brought from its invasion of Poland on September 1, 1939. In 1941, the Nazis performed their experiments with Zyklon B — hydrogen cyanide pills — a chemical preparation designed for use as a pesticide. Cyanide damages the body's cells and prevents the mitochondria from producing the energy required to live. The moment that the Zyklon tablets were exposed to air, they released powerfully deadly, poisonous gas.

In mid-1942, the Nazis evacuated two huts in the town of Auschwitz of the farmers that usually inhabited them and built two temporary gas chambers. The first structure was called Bunker I, or the "little red house" on account of its color. Initially, eight hundred people could be gassed at once. At that time there was only one gas chamber building in the Auschwitz camp. There was also a crematorium called "Crematorium I". To maximize efficiency, the Nazis built a gas chamber in the hut right beside it — Bunker II, called "the little white house," which could kill 1300 victims at once. These were the first two gas chambers in Auschwitz. By June 1943, shipments of prisoners would arrive to train platforms just 2.5 kilometers from the chambers, so the victims were transported on foot or covered trucks directly. Then the railroad tracks were extended, so that three platforms could come as close as possible to the gas chambers.

In 1942, the Nazi extermination apparatus in Auschwitz I moved slowly and in primitive ways. The mass cremation in the pits created thick, pungent smoke that might have betrayed the unthinkable acts which only the greatest of sadists could devise — that which the Nazis established so close to the town of Oswiecim, so close to the cultured Polish city of Krakow.

Some one million, one hundred thousand Jews were murdered in Auschwitz alongside hundreds of thousands of other people that Nazis wanted extinct. It became a symbol of evil and will be remembered as an eternal disgrace, never to be forgiven or forgotten.

Auschwitz II — Birkenau (January 1944 - May 1945)

As Jews continued to flow into Auschwitz from all across Europe, it became necessary to build another camp. And so, at the end of 1941, workers began to build the nearby Birkenau. When the German invasion of Russia (Operation Barbarossa) began on June 22, 1942, creating many Russian prisoners, the camp could not keep up. So the Nazis established the infamous Auschwitz II-Birkenau camp, three kilometers away from the original camp.

Auschwitz-Birkenau was five square kilometers and surrounded by electric fences, four meters tall. The camp was also surrounded by moats, cumulatively 13 kilometers long. Auschwitz-Birkenau was divided into smaller sub-camps. Each camp had a main street where its barracks were built. Electric barbed wire surrounded the prison camps, separating them from one another. There were Postenkette guard posts stationed around the camp and transports arrived ceaselessly. In order to keep up with the number of victims that exponentially grew, the Nazis built four new crematoria, containing 46 ovens which burned over 1,000 victims of the gas chambers daily.

Auschwitz III - Monowitz-Buna Camp

Although Auschwitz was secluded in an area of wetlands, rivers and forests, train access was very convenient. In addition, the large coal reserves in the region's land, the large quantities of water and a reservoir of cheap labor from the Auschwitz I camp made it possible for coal to move the trains. That was one of the reasons why the chemical corporation IG Farben was interested in the possibility of setting up a factory in Buna to produce liquid fuel and synthetic rubber. Thus, east of the town of Oswiecim, south of the town of Monowitz, in the territory annexed by Germany from Poland in 1940, the German conglomerate IG Farben, also known as Buna-Werke, and a network of sub-camps were established.

When the German air strikes on Britain in August and September of 1940 failed, the predictions of a quick victory for the Third Reich were proven wrong. In fall of

1940, when the preparations of Operation Barbarossa began, the German defense minister recommended increasing Buna's annual production to 150,000 tons.

Auschwitz prisoners worked hard labor in the IG Farben factory. More than 100 prisoners were taken to and from work on a truck daily, but as the number of prisoners required to build the factory grew, their numbers grew to several hundred. However their transport was disrupted due to a shortage of trucks, so they were marched, twenty kilometers each way, on foot via a bridge over the Sola River. The long and arduous march hurt the prisoners and their work efficiency. But prisoners' lives had no value to the factory management. The camp was deadly. 25,000 perished in the factory. Citizens of the city who were witnesses to the daily tortures, resented this brutal exploitation of the prisoners. So the Nazis built train tracks over the bridge to carry the prisoners. If the pace of work did not satisfy their bosses, the workers would be beaten with iron bars. The Nazi method was clear — a prisoner unfit for work was unfit for living.

On September 13, 1944, American bombers attacked and partially destroyed the Auschwitz III Buna-Were factory, but evacuation of Auschwitz was postponed for some time because the Allies were busy at that time fighting the war in the Far East against Japan.

Germany was at its most powerful during 1941-1942. It had hundreds of thousands of prisoners in its camps, which it exploited for cheap labor to carry out the dream of the Third Reich. The Jewish prisoners alongside Russian prisoners of war, gypsies and all the other peoples that the Nazis planned to exterminate were put to work doing hard labor and starved within an inch of their lives. As an adolescent, author and Nobel Prize winner Elie Wiesel was a prisoner there along with his father. He did hard labor in the IG Farben factory. Writer and chemist Primo Levi and film director Willie Holt were likewise imprisoned and put to work there.

At its peak, there were 12,000 prisoners working in the rotation. Life expectancy at the camp was 3-4 months.

The trial of Carl Krauch, the chairman of the board of directors, was the sixth trial at Nuremberg. He was sentenced to six years in prison. Various other powerful figures received 'softer' sentences.

The Darkness of Auschwitz

Arriving to Auschwitz, Leibl saw the front Postenkette towers which rose to about twenty meters. The camp was surrounded by electrified barbed-wire fencing roughly four meters tall and above it a bright beam of light illuminated a one-kilometer radius.

While shaking off the overcrowding and the dank air in which he had been trapped on the train for three days, Leibl and the others were ejected from the train car into the brutal cold of winter. The gray sky hung low, heavy and somber over his head. The cold air blew powerfully on his neck and face, making him forget the dense, suffocating air of the train. Arms crossed and desperate, those emerging from the train were hurled into the gaping maw of death.

A doctor, later identified as Dr. Mengele, performed an Aktion: pointing with his fat finger, red and thick like a sausage, he divided the newcomers from the transports into groups. One group for strong men, women and youth whose lives were spared on account of their suitability for work. All the rest — children, women and the elderly were lined up in rows to await their death. Without pause, trucks covered with thick black tarpaulins arrived. The SS soldiers forced the shivering women and children on. Nobody among the truck's passengers knew where they were being taken. Leibl could not take his eyes off them as they were driven away. A thick pipe extended from the trucks' exhaust pipes into the back. As they made their way through the camp, the pipes emitted Zyklon gas into the back, choking all of their passengers. These came to be known as the "black death trucks". Indeed, nobody survived them. The trucks would then stop in front of a deep pit that had been dug earlier and toss the dead cargo into it. An SS officer would then set fire to the pit from each side and soon the victims were engulfed in flames.

As they stood on the Auschwitz platform, the black-uniformed men whipped and abused them mercilessly. Their eyes burned, their nostrils flared, ready to sink their teeth into fresh prey. Beside Leibl stood Berel Sokal.

Suddenly, bleeding and trembling with horror, Berel's six-year-old son Moshe-Himmel sprang toward him and said, "Dad, I want to stay with you."

Berel moved his son into the lineup of men. "Where's

your bread?" asked the father.

"A German hit me with a stick and my bread fell from my hands, but, Dad, I have another slice of bread." The boy tried to encourage him.

When the camp doctor saw this he leaped at the boy. "Heraus!" he cried and threw the boy over onto the railroad tracks. Berel never saw his son again.

From afar, Berel saw his second son, nine-year-old Ichla, in the children's lineup, chewing snow to abate his hunger. Nobody knows where the boy was taken next. Ahead of him, Berel saw his 70-year-old mother standing with her eyes closed, about to fall over. Two Jewish women supported her from either side. His wife was also there awaiting her fate, holding their 18-month-old son Menachemke in her arms. She ran toward her husband to bid him goodbye. "Forgive me," she cried with her remaining strength. She knew that she was nearing death. Then she returned and stood in the women's line. From a distance, Leibl could still see his mother, tears streaming from her eyes, moving deeper into the camp, as guards hit her head, pushing her to keep up with the march. She disappeared from sight. On the ramp in a group of seven, Leibl suddenly saw his sisters, his father, his grandmother and grandfather. His brother Mordechai's wife and her family stood with them too, all close, supporting one another.

Watching his family go, Leibl was paralyzed. He couldn't tear his gaze from them. All at once, his great, big family was meeting its end. Suddenly Leibl felt the blow of a stick to his head. It came from a long-faced Nazi, his nose twitching over his prickly mustache, his lips pursed, his wicked eyes glittering with evil. He hit him over and over again without letting up, robbing him of those final moments of separation from his family. Leibl stood there humiliated, choked with tears, his shoulders trembling, sobbing. Hot tears flowed down his throat. The sky was grim. In the torrential rain, thunder and lightning, they mourned their dead.

All around them, they saw the last round of arrivals to Auschwitz, a line of creatures, bound hand and foot, who did not even look human. Their eyes were dark, as though old age had caught up to them all at once. They were ghostly shadows, and looked long, thin and narrow in the striped pajamas; they looked like skeletons in different sizes. Their skin was dry and cracked. All of them had shaved heads, hip bones protruding, eviscerated, unconscious, still clinging to life, their lips blue and stiff. Their look had a uniformity about it, with similar faces, coats torn, gloveless hands blue with cold. They could barely walk; death followed close behind them. Their teeth and gums showed signs of scurvy. They drank water from an old, rusty tin. The tiny portions of hard bread they received were swallowed quickly. They were unable to drag themselves any further but stubbornly refused to die. "Don't give up," their poor brains told them. "Soon you will get a bit of bread." Although they knew that only death would set them free, they continued on, emaciated, bald and pale as marionettes, trying to match their pace to the healthy so as not to be removed from the ranks of the Auschwitz residents, so that they would not be sent prematurely to the gas chambers.

Through ongoing blows, Leibl, Avraham Berel Sokal, Yisrael Yelin, Ben Shilam, Yankel Delangitch, Bendt Pianco, Shlomo Tanenbaum and Haim Kaviarat and their block neighbors, were separated from the rest of the Auschwitz prisoners. When morning came, with repeated blows to their backs, they were sent out of the blocks and placed in formation for Appell (roll call). Then they were divided into special labor units of two to three hundred laborers. They didn't understand the meaning of the role they were meant to carry out, and nobody bothered to tell them what was expected of them. The Nazis had made them Sonderkommando, a group of prisoners who performed special functions as a secret, separate unit, set apart lest they leak and expose the despicable acts that the Nazis obliged them to perform to the outside world. It quickly became clear to them that they were meant to perform the impossible, monstrous, the most hated and despicable job of all. They were meant to serve as submissive partners in the ongoing process of killing their own people. They were, in fact, running the mass extermination of the Jews. Leibl worked in the factory of death. He spent two years conduction transports of Jews to the gas chambers and incinerators. He did what only the devil would do. For years, after the liberation of Auschwitz and the surrender of the Nazis to the Allies, the work of these men remained clouded in mystery and silence. Few people knew what they had done, and those that did could not believe it.

At the head of each Kommando group was an SS officer and a Kapo under him that guarded them, so they would not lag or evade their work. If any of them were weak or negligent, the officer would send him to his death. Leibl and his friends were participants in the murder industry. They were tasked with carrying out the Nazi concept of eliminating Europe's Jews, a task that was well planned down to the finest detail. They lived and worked in the heart of this hell. Their work was hard, degrading, and full of guilt for the unforgivable sins they committed. They were so despised that everyone in Auschwitz referred to them as the "Crematorium Kommando."

The Gas Chambers

During his first few months in Auschwitz, Leibl worked gathering the clothes. The collection point was about two hundred meters away from the gas chambers and was referred to as "Kanada." It was given this name because it was the impression of Auschwitz residents that Canada was a rich nation, so they named the warehouse that contained all the looted items of jewelry, arts, and all the artifacts of value that the Nazis robbed from the Jews who were brought to slaughter. At first, the workers didn't understand the process that the victims underwent before their death, but together with his friends, as

Leibl would load the objects in wheelbarrows to a central place, he realized the magnitude of the tragedy.

In a big underground building, a room called the "Zonda" served as an undressing room. The room was a few hundred square meters, and two and a half to three meters tall and could hold a thousand victims. While the latter undressed before entering the gas chambers, there was enough time to go through their belongings, gather their food, clothes and valuables that that they had brought with them. Leibl would then take the plundered clothes to the Kanada warehouse.

"Between two rows of our men - the Sonderkommando, equipped with thick sticks, marched the victims to their deaths. We were made to get the victims into that room. We told them that they were standing in line waiting for the cleaning and disinfecting stage of the process, which was why they had had to remove their clothes." Above a bench that ran the length of the concrete wall of the gas chambers, there were racks with racks that served as hangers. Those sentenced to death were told to hang their clothes on a hanger and remember its number. Because after the bathing and disinfecting procedure, when they came out of from the "showers," they could get their clothes back. A sign indicating the way to the showers pointed toward the gas chambers. "We helped them get undressed and unpack the valuables that they had on them. We supplied soap and a towel to a few of them. Their heads were shaved, and socks were produced from the hair for German railroad workers and the lining of shoes for German submarine units. We had to see the naked men and women. Women were examined in their most intimate parts; they were shocked and ashamed. Orthodox women refused to undress before their husbands. We were forced to embarrass them. I avoided looking in their eyes, not wanting to see the face of death as it hovered over the innocent," Leibl confessed.

The Nazis didn't treat their victims as human. The Jews became inferior creatures, humiliated and subhuman, and anyone could do with them as they pleased. "I avoided eye contact. When one of the condemned men snapped at a German, we had to gain control over him and lead him to the gas chamber. We had to avoid any physical contact with them, to refuse their pleas and not to tell them where they were being taken. I was helpless. When I met their eyes, I saw that they knew everything. It killed my spirit."

Mothers clasped their children to them. They held on, hugging their mother around the waist. The child wraps his arms around her and buries his face in her belly. Behind them the father stands close by with his eyes frozen. Their silent cries implored. You could see the face of death. A woman hid her baby in the pile of clothes. One Nazi found the baby and threw him, without pause, into the gas chambers. One woman tried to hide her baby tight against her own body, but he wouldn't stop crying. A Gestapo officer, his eyes glittering, took the small child from her arms and threw him onto the floor of the dressing room.

The winter was as cruel as murder. The room was so cold, the intense chill froze their organs. Even when they realized what was coming for them, they remained exceptionally quiet. One woman, with her eyelids closed, collapsed to the ground. An SS soldier was quick to throw her into the gas chamber. A frenzy took hold of everything. The victims looked like ghosts to me — everyone was grieving. Fear burst from between their ribs, their faces were yellow. I couldn't look them in the eyes when I saw death, which hovered over them, ready to claim them any minute. We pacified them when we could, we assured them that the process would be quick, not to give them time to think. When the condemned asked where the other families were, we had to lie. We tried to comfort them, and we promised that nothing bad would happen to them. We never revealed to the victims what lay before them. Both because we were ordered not to and also out of mercy. I wished I could have been a life raft for them in that hell. I sensed the turmoil within them. Some, as they walked toward the gas chamber, their hands reaching out before them, were like ghosts, groping in the shadows. There was the occasional loud one. A fire of cries poured from them, but God could not hear them. I knew that only death would make them free men again. My friends and I pushed them into the sealed gas chambers. That was how we led them to those defiled gates of death.

Through a corridor that led from the dressing room, we brought the victims in rows of three down the stairs to the basement. Across from the gas chambers was an elevator. Each chamber could contain a thousand victims. The line was long. Some of the Jews were forced to stand in the cold and wait outside the building. Their bodies trembled from the cold, their teeth chattered, their bones rattled against one another. Their feet froze, became numb, standing on the frozen ground which sucked their life force out right through their bare feet. Behind them they could feel the breath of the three people in line behind them. They were confused, their senses growing dim, their walk passive, submissive, embracing one another, they walked together toward the gas chambers. Terror penetrated their hearts. Those who fell down were trampled, nobody tried to resist, as though they accepted their fate, they poured into the trap. Getting a thousand people into the gas chamber took no more than an hour.

The doors of the gas chambers were thick and armored. To ensure that the gas not seep out, we slammed and barred them. Through a hatch in the roof that opened about thirty-five centimeters, SS men poured the Zyklon crystals in - gas in the form of green cubes. Within minutes, the beat of life weakened and went out. It wasn't twenty minutes to poison a thousand people to death. After about half an hour, gestapo would open the back door of the gas chamber. Sometimes the bodies were still warm, quivering, their eyes sunken in their sockets. While our faces were protected by masks, we slowly opened the upper vents of the gas chambers to release the gas that remained. Fans were switched on to remove the hot air saturated with vapor from the chamber. We dragged the corpses away. Due to the frantic struggle and the agony of death, the bodies had undergone a horrific metamorphosis. They were twisted and bent, and their limbs intertwined, tangled with one another, and often fragile.

We lay them on their backs with their faces upwards to make it possible for the team of "dentists" — Jews whose job it was to remove gold teeth from the corpses — to do their work. Sometimes the mouths of the dead were closed so tight that the dentists could not manage to open them, and they were thrown into the crematorium with all their teeth still in their mouths. When the dentists had finished their work, the elevator awaited the victims. Four of us stood at its entrance, two on either side. We dragged the bodies inside. When the elevator reached the landing, the furnaces opened up before us and we threw the bodies inside. The entire killing process from the moment that the Jews arrived at the dressing room until their death took about four hours.

"When we had cleared out the bodies, we had to return to the scene of the crime and ventilate the chambers so that the next victims would not suspect anything bad was going to happen to them. This was how we performed the most terrible, despicable tasks for the Germans."

Many of the Sonderkommando recognized their own relatives among the dead, which was unbearable. These tasks were terrible on Leibl — both physically and emotionally: he could not stand the odors or the fear. He thought that he had lost his sanity, that he was dreaming. Leibl couldn't bear the contempt for human life. Depressed, he froze, watching and experiencing the cruelty all around. He refused to believe what he saw before him, sometimes forgetting that he too was human. "I thought I was dead, or some disappearing shadow. I was in a living hell. I performed my task like someone hypnotized, I became a robot, dehumanized, without feelings, I lost my humanity." He had to numb any pain or emotion just to survive the moment, the hour, to not despair completely. To bow down and carry out some action, to perform his gruesome work. "I grew cynical and sealed myself off from my surroundings. I forgot what I had done. It became routine, I developed indifference — evidently you can get used to anything. I was in an exhausting daily struggle. Did I have a choice? To this day I can't forget what I did. It still torments me, even though I was forced, I decided that I would not fall prey to the hands of the Nazis."

After the burning, the SS soldiers returned to the "zonda" where they looted the dead of everything that remained behind: glasses, rings and other items. They took the stolen property to the Kanada warehouse where the treasure accumulated. Sometimes trucks were seen waiting at the entrance to the warehouse while prisoners loaded them with the looted treasure. The heavy trucks made their way to Germany where they awaited distribution among the Nazi dignitaries. The looters claimed that in so doing they raised the morale on the home front — but the average German civilians did not gain anything from this either.

Among other things, the satanic Nazi who commanded Auschwitz wrote about the Sonderkommando in his autobiography, "Some among the Sonderkommando even discovered their own family members among the dead, or those led into the chambers. While this may be shocking, there was never any resulting incident. I was witness to one such time: while removing the bodies from the chambers, suddenly one of the Sonderkommando began to tremble and froze momentarily, but then he went on pulling out the bodies along with his friends. I asked the

Kapo what was going on with him. The Kapo inquired and found that the Jew shook when he discovered his wife among the bodies. I went to keep an eye on him, but there was nothing out of the ordinary. He went on dragging the bodies as before. When I returned again sometime later, the Sonderkommando was sitting and eating among the others as though nothing had happened. What gives the Jews the strength to do this gruesome workday and night? Were they hoping for some act that would save them from death? Or did their senses grow dim with horror until they didn't even have the strength to end it and save themselves from this reality? But it never became clear to me."

In the 1980s in Israel, when the work that was so despicable as to be confidential was discovered, Leibl told his wife and children what he experienced and was forced to do during his two years of imprisonment in Auschwitz. He told them the worst — that he and his friends were forced to do the most monstrous, impossible, despicable, hateful job of all; how he was tasked with taking an active part in the extermination apparatus. The Sonderkommando group carried out the Nazi extermination plan and aided them with their own hands. They were practiced in the operation of the elaborate, carefully designed system of murder that only a frightful, truly evil mind could come up with. But Leibl didn't tell his family about the benefits he enjoyed as a member of the Sonderkommando. He didn't tell them how the SS turned a blind eye when he and his friends took food and liquor from the victims' belongings that they found in the zonda. In general, the Sonderkommando unit was infinitely better off than Auschwitz' other prisoners, and, as the Auschwitz survivor and Sonderkommando Josef Zucker testified, "We didn't experience shortage — neither in food nor clothing. We didn't suffer starvation or sleeplessness, we had clothes and shoes that whole time. We were the only ones to enjoy such privileges, the rest of the prisoners couldn't even dream of having it so good. Our block's conditions were exceptional."

The privileges that the Nazis gave the Sonderkommando were sometimes even better than what the SS men received. Their block was outside the area for the rest of the prisoners and there was no contact between them. Members of the Sonderkommando unit lived above the crematoria, which heated the building on the harsh winter nights. They slept on straw mats with blankets and pillows. They wore regular clothes rather than the striped attire of the other Auschwitz prisoners. While others perished from cold and hunger, they had reasonable living conditions.

Sometimes Leibl got lucky and was given a shift working in the Kanada Warehouse. In a rectangular yard, fenced in by barbed wire and about two hundred meters from the gas chambers, stood huge warehouses that contained valuables: paintings by famous painters, gold bullion and gold jewelry, diamonds and cash. These items piled up. Kanada was a kind of paradise for the Sonderkommando, as they could take any of the foods — bread, margarine, butter, preserved meats, salami sandwiches, chocolate. There was lots of everything. It often seemed to them that Jews had been taken mid-meal. There was food fresh from the plates of prisoners, which was why other Auschwitz inmates called them the "clean-up commando."

In Leibl's first months in Auschwitz, he worked collecting the clothing that was taken from the victims about to enter the gas chambers. The stolen property was gathered in the warehouse. Leibl saw hundreds of brightly colored baby carriages, looking unused as if they had been just bought for a first child. These carts had belonged to wealthy Jews and were evidence of their owners' wealth. There were used baby carriages too, but no babies.

The Sonderkommando threw hundreds of suitcases, boxes, bags, backpacks and packages into this warehouse, and they piled up in the center of the space. Next to the warehouse rose a mountain of some 50-100 thousand confiscated down quilts. Another stockpile contained pots and pans pilfered from thousands of kitchens.

Into the warehouse, they unpacked the suitcases, the boxes and packs, emptied them onto an enormous blanket. They poured jewelry, textiles, furs, perfumes, art and more out sorted them into piles. The personal documents and family photos that were found among the belongings had to be burned. From among the Jewish prisoners, they selected photos of elegant, shapely, healthy, well-dressed women. Those women were the candidates to sort through the items and pack the loot into bundles. Several women emptied toothpaste tubes. The Nazis worried that the Jews hid jewelry, diamonds and other valuables inside.

Empty trains would arrive close to the Kanada warehouse, and the workers would load them with the stolen goods. The items were sorted according to value. Every package sent to Germany contained items of a certain sort. Then it was sent to Germans at the front to boost their morale.

Nearly twenty Sonderkommando sorted goods in Kanada. "Kanada commando" was by far the best work. Although they seemed calm, its workers were proud of the easy, rewarding work they were given. They felt guilty that in the midst of the Nazi inferno they were living like relative kings. "But the guilt is not ours; it is that of those who forced us to do such work," he concluded.

However, the SS men were always standing by, keeping close watch on the "death workers." If one of them didn't meet their demands, he would be whipped then pushed into the gas chambers. Anyone who stumbled or fell was not spared. They were simply trampled.

In these humiliating and despicable circumstances, full of guilt for his unforgivable deeds, Leibl bowed his head and performed his role as though transfixed. He had to go on surviving each moment, each hour. "To this day, I can't believe the things I saw with my own eyes." Amazingly, despite their unthinkable suffering, nobody among them took his own life. They were so despised, that sometimes they felt their fortune was no better than those that they had to kill.

But the Sonderkommando didn't have much time either. The units worked in rotations. Each cycle numbered around two to four hundred prisoners. In order that their secret labor not be discovered and so as not to leave any eyewitnesses to the crime and Eichmann's orders at the end of their service, most of the Sonderkommando were eventually executed. Their bodies were evacuated by their replacements on the same route by which they themselves had previously led their victims. A new commando unit that arrived directly from the Jewish terminus in the next transport replaced them. Leibl and his group's operations went on for about two years. At its peak, the Sonderkommando unit numbered three thousand four hundred forced laborers. Only eighty of them survived up until the camp's liberation by the Allies.

According to testimony from Auschwitz commandant,

Rudolf Hoss, before his trial in Warsaw, only skilled workers such as those who manned the furnaces, mechanics and other inmates with important jobs were left alive.

"Life expectancy in Auschwitz did not exceed six months. Out of the approximately 2,500 Wysokie residents who were imprisoned at Auschwitz from January 1942 until January 1944, only 20 survived. Among them were myself and my friends Moshe Brenner, Avraham Berel Sokal, Lazar Gaskovitz and Moshe Yossel Kassiar," Leibl concluded.

"It's no wonder that I refused to speak for all those years about what I experienced; I wasn't willing to shine any light onto my despicable experience. While I was doing those things, a part of my soul died. But we, the Sonderkommando, didn't murder Jews; it was the Nazis who murdered them. We were just the enemy's slaves."

CHAPTER 8

The "Union" and the Rebellion

The parent factory of the "union" — Weichsel Metall-Union Werk — produced weapons on the grounds of the Auschwitz-Birkenau camp for about a year before it was evacuated in early 1945 at the start of the Russian offensive. Later in its operations, there were five hundred girls working the dayshift and another five hundred working the nightshift. Each shift was 12 hours long. The walk from the camp to the factory took about an hour in any weather. On their way, the girls, aged 18-20, passed by the crematoria and the appalling sight of naked bodies being thrown into them.

The factory exists to this day, presently located in Germany's industrial Ruhr region, in a small town called Frondenberg. Today they produce chains and other motorcycle parts. It is prosperous and successful.

When the Germans were defeated, the parent factory remained intact. Its owner, Fritz Schrepper, returned from Auschwitz to his factory in Frondenberg and continued to work there for decades without ever having to account for his crimes, as though nothing had happened. He never even stood before a panel for justice, the kind denouncing the Nazis and those who helped them. He returned, worked and operated the factory until his death at a ripe old age.

After the war, when people visited the town and spoke with its residents, they asked about the factory. When Fritz Schrepper's name was mentioned, the residents immediately responded, "Ah! The executioner from Auschwitz." That was how they remembered the evil man. The person who discovered the later existence of the factory was a Jew named Ernest Cohen who, as a prisoner at Auschwitz, had worked in the factory's secretariat. At the end of the war, Cohen worked to memorialize the crimes committed there, and organized a memorial service. Indeed, to this day the place bears a sign with the words "*Weichsel Metall-Union — Here, on January 6, 1945, five of the factory workers were hanged before all the prisoners.*" The ceremony was attended by two survivors of the "union" who came from Israel, representatives of the German establishment, hundreds of school children, heads of local authority, and the media. Ashamed, nobody from the "Union" came to show their respects.

During the war, throughout the grueling work hours, Fritz Schrepper would walk between the machines, keeping a close eye on everything and woe be the girl who dallied at her work. It happened on more than one occasion, as it would happen in any factory, that a machine had some problem and stopped working. Schrepper would then roar and rage at the bloody Jews sabotaging the machines and immediately complained to the Gestapo to establish order.

Nobody noticed that beside the union building were those Jewish prisoners who did the most terrible work of all. These were men from the special Sonderkommando unit. At the edge of the factory, under the skies of Auschwitz, stood crematoria and killing machines where Leibl and his friends worked. They were sent most nights to the women's blocks to gather the corpses of those women who had died in the night of illness and starvation. Often as many as 200 corpses would be collected on a nightshift.

At the beginning of October 1944, when the Wehrmacht suffered defeat after defeat on Russian soil in Operation Barbarossa, transports to Auschwitz slowed down and the incinerators slowed as well. This was an indication to the Sonderkommando that their numbers were about to be thinned. It was also known Nazi policy that live witnesses to their actions and crimes should not be left alive. Every three months, SS men, imbued with Nazi ideology would murder a Sonderkommando detachment, numbering hundreds of men, and force them into the crematoria with their own people. In place of the obliterated squadron, the Nazis brought a new Jewish transport straight off the train to Auschwitz of young, sturdy men. These men would then serve as the new Sonderkommando.

Rumors around Auschwitz reported that the Red Army from the East and the Allied armies were approaching Poland and would close in on German forces like a vise. The Wehrmacht had already taken its last steps in defeat, so the Sonderkommando knew that the Nazis were about to throw hundreds of men from among their ranks into the furnaces with the intention of covering their tracks and hiding evidence of their actions.

The union workers and Sonderkommando men decided that rebellion was in order; there was little to lose. A factory worker by the name of Roza Robota was the contact person with the Sonderkommando. Guta Blau, who had been among the first batch of young women sent to work in the union at the beginning of its organization, even before the production of explosives for the German war machine began, was one of the rebellion's leaders.

In one of the union divisions they produced pots and bowls. The Sonderkommando who, as a result of the nature of their work, were detached from the rest of the camp inmates, managed to make contact with the worker Roza Robota, who managed the girls. In coordination with Israel Gutman and Yehuda Laufer, who worked at the union, and under their guidance, the girls installed double bottoms on the plate ware they produced. In the space created between the bottom and the false bottom, they collected and hid gunpowder that had been produced in the factory. Each evening, as they returned from work, the girls would hand over the gunpowder that they had collected to Roza Robota. When the Sonderkommando visited them, Roza equipped them with the valuable material. The men hid the material inside their carts — among the corpses they had gathered. Then they moved it to a hiding place beside the furnaces. Leibl kept a stash of the explosives for himself. It accumulated in its hiding place until it became a significant amount. Then the men passed it along to some Auschwitz inmates, a Polish Jew by the name of Robel and a Russian technician named Borodin, who fashioned a handmade hand grenade from it. Forbski, the electrician, served as a liaison between the underground and the Union. This collection work continued until it was possible to carry out the crazy idea that burned in their bones — to set the Auschwitz-Birkenau incinerators on fire. Helpless and hopeless, the girls decided to put a stop to, or at least damage, the Nazi killing machine. Together with the men, they organized themselves as a group that was ready to sacrifice their own lives for this higher purpose.

After some time, the Nazis discovered the cache of gunpowder. Without delay, the group of men, death hovering close around them, decided that this was their moment to rise up. They were ready to put their troubles behind them.

The rebellion was planned for Saturday, October 7, 1944. The group decided: "Let us die with the Philistines". There were those who discouraged taking action, saying, "Even if you set fire to everything, where are you going to run? They'll kill you right away." Mordecai, Leibl's brother, who worked in the sewer, collaborated with the rebels. Leibl led the rebellion. A Polish prisoner named Yozik joined him, as well as a Jew named David, and another friend from Wysokie Mazowickie, Mordecai Gravinski. Dozens of men from the Sonderkommando also joined in.

In the uprising, which lasted 12 hours, four hundred and fifty-one Sonderkommando took part. It was carried out in several places at once: In the yard of Crematorium III, a prisoner approached an SS soldier and hit him on the head with a hammer. The soldier fell to the ground. Other rebels attacked and fell upon Kapo Kroll and threw him, live, into the burning furnace. The rebels caught other SS men and threw them into the incinerator. Jewish men beat other SS soldiers with improvised weapons — knives, rocks, steel rods, axes, hammers and homemade grenades. There were those who attacked the Germans with just their hands and in so doing managed to kill another three SS — Willy Priza, Yozef Furka and Rudolf Ehrler — and injure still more. The rebels snuck into the crematorium building and began, with the help of rags doused in flammable liquid, to set fire to the mattresses in the attic above the incinerators. With hand grenades and other tools filled with gunpowder they managed to blow up one of the incinerators. Clouds of smoke rose and turned the sky dark gray, until the building collapsed completely. Two chimneys and iron rods collapsed. Rioting, they set fire to and burned up the fourth incinerator which was never used again.

With scissors, many rebels cut the electric fence, which was only operational at night, and began to escape. Within nine kilometers of the camp perimeter, all of them had been shot dead by Nazi guards. Mordecai, Leibl's brother, along with others, made it eight kilometers before reaching a hayloft. There the Germans surrounded them, set the hayloft on fire and killed all the Kommando men who had escaped into it, apart from Leibl who managed to flee, though his brother remained behind. The Jews, Auschwitz prisoners who didn't understand what was happening around them, ran around the camp yard in a panic. Some wandered naively around the camp and were shot in the commotion. One after another they dropped, wounded or dead, to the ground. "These were added to the hundreds of fighters that were lost," testified Sonderkommando Philip Miller.

Four hundred and fifty-one Sonderkommandos were killed in the uprising. Only two hundred and twelve of them remained alive. The Nazis did not discover Leibl's participation. He was questioned but left to carry on his work. His friend Lazar was also questioned and survived. That was the one and only uprising of its sort that took place in Auschwitz.

On January 6, 1945, not long before the Russian advance and the evacuation of Auschwitz, it was announced over the factory's loudspeakers: "Inmates conspired to damage and blow up the crematorium. Gunfire for explosion was also stolen by union workers and they will be punished." A cruel, prolonged investigation only led to five of the girls who had participated in the uprising. Roza Robota, responsible for gathering the gunpowder, had been their leader. She was the one who coaxed and encouraged the other prisoners to rebel. Ella Gartner, Ester Wajcblum, Regina Safirsztain were all arrested, questioned and tortured, but they did not offer any details.

That same day — three weeks before Auschwitz was liberated by the Red Army, beside Dr. Mengele's house of experiments — the gallows were placed. Before all the prisoners of Auschwitz, the union girls who waited for their death were forced to stand in the square without detracting from the spectacle of the hanging of their friends until it was their turn to mount the gallows. In the center of the camp the Nazis first hung Roza Robota who, moments before her death, cried: "Revenge!" And the nineteen-year-old Ester Wajcblum went to her death with her head held high. Two of the suspects who finished the nightshift and made their way to their barracks were led directly to the gallows. Another worker was brought there at the end of her dayshift.

Although Guta Blau was one of the organizers of the revolt, the Germans did not suspect her of collaborating, so she was spared the noose. Several months earlier when she was a prisoner at Majdanek, Guta had been one among a group of women brought into the Zonda hall — the undressing room before the entering the gas chambers. She was required to undress before the "rinse" in order to be "disinfected." Before going to her death, Guta cried out "Shema Yisrael," and when her turn came to enter the gas chambers with her friends, the execution was delayed for a long time. The women, without knowing the reason for the delay, waited for their death in the gas chamber, for the Zyklon B to begin to flow. Suddenly an SS man opened the door and Guta and her friends, naked, trembling in the terrible cold and nerves, but alive, fled the scene. The reason for the delay, as it turned out afterward, was that the Zyklon gas, which was supposed to poison the women, had run out. Guta Blau survived the Holocaust, emigrated to Israel and was married. In 1990, Guta Blau-Kaufman died in Tel Aviv.

Despite the failure of the uprising, which was to be expected, the friends remained strong in their beliefs and refused to give up. They decided to resume their rebellion at the appropriate time. It was an unprecedented initiative which, even if its outcome had been known in advance, was a kind of victory for human morality; the fighting back of the prisoners who had not yet lost their humanity, nor all hope.

Roza Robota's story was unknown in Israel until Eichmann's trial. She was deported to Auschwitz in 1942. At first, she worked in the clothing heaps of the Kanada warehouse and later was sent to work in the "union" factory. In his testimony, Israel Gutman spoke of her heroism. The writer Haim Gouri and other journalists who reviewed the trial also spoke of her strength of character and heroism.

CHAPTER 9

Confession and Condemnation

April 11, 1961. A major event is happening in our lifetime: at the International Convention Center in Jerusalem, the haunting, hair-raising stories of dozens of Holocaust survivors are being told, testifying before the court on the crimes of Adolf Eichmann, who sits in his armored glass cage for protection.

We were at home, tense, listening closely to the sound coming from the box — a Philips radio receiver. In the middle of the receiver is a round speaker — a perforated mesh draped with thick linen cloth, and an accumulation of dust. Three gold buttons are bolted, in a line, to its front; one regulates the volume, another tries to tune into the only broadcast network we have. The third stands silent, waiting for the day some other radio channel would open up to diversify the content available to us.

Suddenly, the thick voice of the Attorney General Gideon Hausner booms from the device, inviting Holocaust survivors to come and give their testimony. At home we were anxiously craning our necks toward the device, trying to hear everything. Suddenly we were all gripped by fear. Over the airwaves came the voice of a witness — our close friends Leibl. Only now — 16 years since he had survived the Holocaust, did we learn from his testimony the worst thing imaginable — that Leibl had been in the Sonderkommando unit at Auschwitz.

On the witness' stand, Leibl told his story of his meeting with Eichmann; how the terrible man hurried Leibl and his friends to clear the bodies out of the gas chambers and into the incinerators. Leibl's story and testimony of his encounter with Eichmann made my parents shiver and shake. Mom broke down in tears. Dad remained frozen where he stood. Moisture filled his blue eyes that I loved so much. They turned gray then black, sinking into their sockets.

That same evening Leibl came to our house, as if to explain, or perhaps to apologize for and to tell my parents his mysterious stories.

"All those years I refused to talk about what I experienced, what I saw with my own eyes," he began. "I couldn't, I repressed it and refused to shed any light on those hellish two years of my life. My world was despicable. I was despised by others. My soul was broken. Sometimes I forgot that I was human. I thought that I was dead or just an invisible ghost in the chaos of Auschwitz. I cooperated with inhuman sadism. Can you even understand the extent of my predicament? My personal values crumbled entirely, but how could I ignore their desecration? I was just a cog in the death machine of Auschwitz, a cog that helped the Nazis in exterminating my own people. I see myself pushing the carts of suffocated Jews, throwing them into the gaping maw of the incinerators. Other inmates called us 'furnace reapers'. Could anyone understand how I could stand it, could cope with the harrowing experience and abuse, cruelty and hostility? I experimented with inhumanity. The amount of cynicism that it took for me to destroy my people… I thought I had lost my mind. I thought that I was dreaming. I couldn't think anymore, as though my brain had stopped working. All I wanted then was to go on living, to survive the next hour, the next second. My distress weighed on me, overpowered me, will never be alien to me. I had no choice but to act in the darkness that was Birkenau. I lost the capacity for emotion. All I wanted was to numb any feeling, all pain. At night I still see myself scraping the ash of my friends and family from the crematoria, the sacred ash of those who were once Jews, and throwing it into the Sola River. The river rose up angry, flooding, shrouded in black. I was young, eager and optimistic; I didn't understand the atmosphere of murder, the evil and the death all around me. I was imprisoned by Nazi talons. I knew there was no escape from it. I feared the extent of the torture my body would have to endure. But I adjusted to the horror, became an automaton. With indifference and routine, I carried out my work. I lost my humanity. Man can grow accustomed to anything. I became indifferent, forgot what I was doing, the nature of my work. It became routine. I tried to block out any feeling, or pain, but the will to live, not to give up, took hold of me and kept me from losing my mind entirely. In survival, a person can become as heartless as any animal. Not once did death stop breathing down my neck; he looked right at me. I knew that the day was not far off when he would pull me to him. When I was first assigned to the Sonderkommando unit, my more experienced friends said, "Everything is better here than in the other Auschwitz barracks. But you should know — none of us leaves here alive." But I hoped that one day it would all be over. How long could the Nazis go on like this? Someone would have to put an end to it.

"In order to keep us quiet, so we would not leak information of our actions and to suppress our rebellion we, the Sonderkommando, had the best living conditions of all of Auschwitz' prisoners. Our world went on as usual, living in the attic of Crematorium I. On cold winter nights, it warmed our sleep. I had a good bed with a blanket and pillow. We had warm clothes. We could shower daily with hot water above the crematorium, while Jews were being burned beneath us. Indeed, there was no contact between those of us above and the rest of the prisoners of Auschwitz.

"The food we received was plentiful and high quality. We ate the food that remained, left over from the dead, food from the Jews that had been taken straight to the gas chambers. Sometimes there was even vodka we could drink. The guards joined us in eating. Every day we got a portion of meat. There were leftovers. We didn't know what to take. We had Sonderkommando among us whose senses had grown dim, made them primitive and brutish. My eyes too avoided seeing the reality I was living in and what I was doing. The rest of the Auschwitz inmates claimed that we became indifferent to what we were doing. They had all kinds of derogatory names for us, like 'furnace reapers' or 'body draggers.' They hated us fiercely, as if we were doing it of our own free will. I had no choice but to adapt. I quickly became cynical, closed off from myself and my surroundings. An automatization process began within me. I worked like a robot. I got used to my work, but this daily, exhausting struggle came with despair and suicide. There were those among us who had lost their minds and lay down on the wire fences. Death saved them from their agony.

"Everyone treated us as subhuman; they claimed that we were physically cruel and violent in bringing the victims to the gas chambers. The fear that no one would understand that we did those terrible things because we were forced and abused by the Nazis, added another dimension to my suffering. The fact that the world after Auschwitz wouldn't understand tormented me.

"How could I share any of this with Lotte and the kids? Would they have understood? Would they have blamed me? Indeed, the work I did was sinful. My heart is full of regret for things that cannot be forgiven. I accompanied those condemned to death through each stage of their destruction. Would they understand the shame that tormented me in the face of thousands of children, women and men stripping off their clothes in the 'sauna' moments before I shoved them into the gas chambers? You know how I could stand the pleas of the victims, asking me to tell them what to expect in the next twenty minutes? I knew that when I was made to do this cursed work and doomed thus to die, that the secret of the 'final solution' was held within me.

"We worked in rotations. Every few months the Nazis would execute three to four hundred men from our unit, so that we would not be able to tell the outside world of their actions. In place of the Sonderkommando who had just been sent to the furnaces, the Nazis brought carefully selected Jewish prisoners from the latest transports that arrived in Auschwitz. It was a new unit of hearty Jewish men who did not know what was expected of them. As the Jewish people dwindled, it meant that the Nazis no longer needed so many Sonderkommando — that their lives too were on the verge of extinction. I was a candidate for death without knowing when my turn would come, but even though I was submissive and beleaguered, I decided that they would not kill me.

"I was a prisoner in Auschwitz for three years. My last day was January 18, 1945, when I was taken out to the death march with thousands of other survivors. From the two years and twelve cycles of Sonderkommando men, amounting to about five thousand, only twenty of us remained at the time of liberation. Until today, no matter where I go, I am accompanied by death. I will always carry that stain on my heart. But we — the Sonderkommando units — were not murderers. The Nazis were the murderers."

I, Sarah, was 14 years old at the time I heard this story. As Leibl spoke, my parents tried to protect me from the terrible things he was telling them, and many times instructed me to go to bed. But I, fascinated, refused to leave the living room, until Dad scolded me, saying that Leibl would stop talking until I went to sleep. I gave in and left them with their secret, pretending to go to my room. But I didn't really give in, I stood behind the living room door, listening intently to all the details. From the dawn of my childhood, I have been in awe and horror of the Holocaust, and the story of the Sonderkommando often disturbed me.

Certain writers and thinkers tend to describe them in a negative light: the controversial Jewish historian Hannah Arendt developed unusual theories and ideas about the Sonderkommando. She says that to this day they feel isolated and denied their identity. It's hard for them to break away from the past. It is as though their actions murdered their personhood.

Her extreme opinions were not without prejudice, as if her eyes were dim, thus avoiding seeing the impossible reality that prevailed at Auschwitz at the time. She claimed that the Sonderkommando were involved in the process without resistance. As though they were running the death machine of their own free will and committing criminal acts to save their own skin. She also claimed that the Nazis chose undesirable characters from Jewish society, imposing upon and damning them with the despicable work. According to Arendt, they were chosen for their talents, strength, and degree of cruelty. She ignores the fact that the Sonderkommando were prisoners whose lives were at stake.

In the 1960s, as they were beginning to be discovered, most of the Israeli public reacted negatively to the Sonderkommando. They were condemned, stuck with the label of collaborators and traitors. The public thought of them in the same category as the Judenrat and the Kapos, who also, by virtue of their jobs, were suspected of gaining advantage and exploiting their status and in so doing cooperated with the Nazis. It was alleged that they were afraid to reveal their secret even to their families because of the guilt and shame.

So they were alone in coping with the nightmares that haunted them for the rest of their lives. They had to suppress the trauma and the disturbing memories. Getting back to life was very difficult. The agony of conscience and fear would not let them be. They encountered suspicion and skepticism and could not share it with anyone from their past. Perhaps if their closest friends had known, they might have been supportive.

But perhaps because of the public shame and discomfort, or maybe because of the scant compassion and understanding of the public toward them, the subject was not prominent in the press in the sixties, as though a web of silence had been established in the country. But there were people with a certain understanding and even those who had compassion for them. And indeed, until the end of the eighties, Israeli society was not ready to look at their past without judging their actions, but after the film *Holocaust* by Claude Lanzmann in 1985, there was a change in public perspective. The Sonderkommando grew willing to reveal their identities in press and documentaries. Even so, to this day, Israeli society remains wary.

My relations to Leibl were ambivalent. I knew him my entire life. He was a dedicated best friend to my parents. I knew all the stories of heroism and battle that had taken place in the ghetto and the period when my parents were forced to hide in the fields and forests. I knew how my father and grandfather split the last bit of bread. For me, Leibl was a beloved and revered character. I understood that if he had refused to carry out what was demanded of him in Auschwitz, some other Jew would have taken his place. I understood that even if he had been so desperate as to kill himself, there would have been no shortage of Sonderkommando thanks to him. I was familiar with his optimistic spirit. I knew that the entire time he was in Auschwitz, he believed that the day was fast approaching, as eventually it did, when he and the rest of the prisoners would be released by the Allied Forces. I try not to judge anybody if I can't put myself in his shoes. And who can imagine living in the reality of the Sonderkommando? Can a person really stay alert when doing things your brain cannot conceive?

Finally, in autumn of 1944, the Sonderkommando rebelled and tried to break out of Auschwitz-Birkenau. Four SS soldiers were killed and 451 Sonderkommando were shot to death.

Leibl died of old age in 1998 on the kibbutz where he had made his life, a gracious man.

CHAPTER 10

Liquidation of Auschwitz and the Death March

Contrary to the nonaggression pact signed on September 23, 1939 between Ribbentrop and Molotov — the German and Soviet foreign ministers, respectively, the German Wehrmacht along with the Axis powers (Nazi Germany, fascist Italy and their satellite states of Romania, Hungary and Finland) invaded the USSR on June 22, 1941, in an attack known as Operation Barbarossa. The destructive war took the lives of some 20 million soldiers and civilians.

In February 1943, there was a turnaround in the battles when the Red Army forced the Nazis to withdraw. In heroic face-to-face combat, the Red Army managed to hold Moscow, its capital, while expelling the Wehrmacht from Russian territory. The Allied armies closed in on Nazi forces from the west, while the Red Army from the east.

The war that had destabilized all of Europe lasted four years, from June 22, 1941, until January 1945 when the German Army was defeated by the Russian winter, unable to stand the fierce cold. And so began the end of the Third Reich, and the extermination camps "breathed" their last breath. By now, the Allied Forces were at the door of the Auschwitz-Birkenau camp. The Nazis knew that they posed an existential threat and would want revenge. And indeed, on May 5, 1945, Auschwitz stopped "breathing" entirely. "We were afraid to leave Auschwitz. We knew what it was, but we did not know what other dangers lay in our path when we left," said Leibl.

In fact the Russian winter ("General Winter") was the cause of the fall and retreat of the Germans. In February 1943, Germany's Sixth Army under the command of Paulus surrendered to the Soviet Union. They then began to mobilize to evacuate the concentration and extermination camps that were in danger of falling to the Red Army.

Hitler did not learn his lesson from the outcome of the war of Emperor Napoleon Bonaparte, who in 1812, about

124 years earlier, had invaded Russia with his army of some 400,000 soldiers. In that bloody invasion, "General Winter" defeated the Napoleonic army which could not stand the weather conditions, the snow and cold that ruled Russia throughout its harsh winter, forcing the French Army to withdraw from Russian soil.

"We heard the explosions of the American Air Force, but we couldn't see the planes themselves. We only saw the Russian bombers, shelling constantly. Many SS soldiers were killed and despite the fire, through which one couldn't discern between the enemies and their victims, dozens of prisoners were also wounded. The noise from the air was causing mayhem and panic among the SS."

Helplessly they ran in every direction — around the camp and around one another, hiding from the heavy shelling. The commanders gave conflicting orders. Wehrmacht soldiers were called to save the day. But when they understood that their officers were no longer anywhere to be seen, having run for their lives, the SS guards left their posts and began to defect and flee. Mostly they were shot by other commanders who were still at their posts. SS units disbanded and scattered everywhere. The retreat was at its peak. When the area was free of officers, the SS men began to run wild and rob everything the prisoners had. They took over the property of the Poles who lived in the nearby villages. "I never imagined that I would see those troops at their lowest," said Leibl triumphantly. "I'll never forget the sight of hundreds of Germans fleeing just as we fled. All of them looked the same. The heroes fled on horse-drawn carriages and on foot. They looked as pathetic as we had."

Himmler feared that the Red Army would soon conquer Auschwitz without the camp commander Rudolf Hoss having time to destroy the damning evidence. So he instructed that they stop the extermination by gas and destroy the gas chambers and incinerators. Indeed, it stopped completely. He then ordered that all the paperwork that had accumulated in the SS offices be burned. Flaming shreds of paper clippings filled the skies of Auschwitz. But in the commotion, Polish inmates managed to get their hands on some documents that would later provide evidence of the horrors to the world.

Now the Nazis were left with hundreds of their prisoners who roamed the camp without SS control. Now the Nazis were being attacked, afraid for their lives. All remaining residents of Auschwitz were living witnesses to what had happened in the death camp. The Nazis wanted to be rid of their human burden in any way possible — before their power ran out. Hoss decided to put them to work at hard labor in the Nazi war machine. He instructed them to be removed from Auschwitz-Birkenau, to forcibly march them over huge distances, with inhuman conditions. This march came to be known as the "death march". The order was to shoot any prisoner that tried to escape from formation or began to lag behind in the march.

"So as to leave no witnesses to what we had done under their command," Leibl said, "the Nazis began to distribute a large amount of gunpowder between the barracks where we lived, hoping that the fire would trap and consume us. They hoped that none of us would survive and there would be no witnesses to the acts they forced us — the Sonderkommando — to do.

"The five of us — Moshe Brenner, Avraham Berel-Sokal, Lazar Gaskovitz, Moshe Yossel Kassiar and I — were given the task of dismantling the chimneys of the crematoria, to obscure and burn anything that might be discovered and revealed by the Allies. We had to pile dirt, cover and fill the pits into which victims' bodies had been cast. We also had to gather the huge number of belongings that had accumulated in the Kanada warehouse and load it onto train cars to be taken to Germany. We were ordered to burn all property that we did not manage to get rid of.

"The Polish gendarmerie, collaborators with the Nazis, also took part in dismantling the crematoria. Clouds of smoke rose up from the furnaces. Bits of doors and windows, pulled from their frames, were strewn everywhere. They set fire to every building and structure of their headquarters. While we were taking apart the chimneys, we heard the crematoria explode one after another," said Leibl.

"The shooting began immediately after exiting the camp's gates. The German guards killed each prisoner that faltered. The road was strewn with dead bodies. Their blood dyed the snow red. At night they would stow us among Polish homes of families who, fearing for their lives, had fled in all directions, leaving their houses and yards behind. The Nazi killing increased as our strength dwindled. Anyone who fell on the way was shot. Thirty percent of the prisoners died or were killed in less than a week. Alongside the roads of Silesia were mass graves for those who died on the march from Auschwitz. After the war, the corpses of thousands of prisoners who had frozen to death were discovered.

"On January 15, 1945, at 4:00 in the morning, with no explanation, we were taken out, under heavy guard, Moshe Brenner, Avraham Berel-Sokal, Lazar Gaskovitz, Moshe Yossel Kassiar and me and thousands of other prisoners to the main square of Auschwitz-Birkenau. We were attached to a long convoy of prisoners that made their way by foot, train, trucks, and horse-drawn carriage toward ruined Germany. It was a multitude of hungry, exhausted people, shuffling their feet, wading through mud or on sleighs. Battalions of prisoners, one hundred in each group, were arranged in rows of five. Six armed guards accompanied each. The Jewish prisoners marched at the front, followed by German political prisoners, then the Russian prisoners."

There did not appear to be any settlements in the surrounding area. Along the way were heaps of corpses

— those who could not stand the conditions. Thus the prisoners were marched without stopping and without purpose or aim. Alongside those who were not yet exhausted, were the *muselmanner*, the "walking dead," moving with no power, falling face first into the earth, breathing their last breaths.

"We wore only summer clothes, tattered rags, no socks, and torn shoes. On the way I found a pair of wooden shoes that had been left behind from some other transport. They were too big for me, but I trudged along in them the entire way. There were clothes to be found along the way, too, but we did not touch them. They were contaminated by the blood of the victims who had last worn them. My frozen fingers were paralyzed. I could no longer hold onto the handles of the sled that sometimes passed me by, with some of their passengers frozen dead. My underwear were very damp. I shook. My neck and shoulders became stiff and cramped. I was so exhausted that every movement became excruciating. But the will to live gave me the power to jump, pound my hands and shoulders to warm up and get rid of the chunks of ice that had piled up on me. An indifferent sun popped out occasionally and warmed my back a little, but immediately gave way to gloomy clouds that weighed heavily on my soul. The mountains looked out over us, tall and silent. God was nowhere to be found," added Leibl.

In the cities of eastern Prussia there were heartbreaking *scenes of horror:* wrecked churches going up in flames, corpses and carcasses lying side by side in the streets and among the rubble, trucks and automobiles scorched and overturned. The violence and murder did not spare elders, women or children. In most towns, almost all of the girls and women were raped, regardless of their age.

"The appearance of the prisoners was haunting. We were weary and weak with hollow, frightened faces, wearing rags that barely covered their scrawny bodies. We shook with cold as the temperature went below ten degrees centigrade. My wooden clogs not only did not provide warmth but made me even colder with their shape and hardness which caused blisters and sores on my feet.

"At the start of the journey, each prisoner received 500 grams of bread and 120 grams of margarine. After that we did not receive any more food or drink. We could not bear the cruelty. It was beyond what we could endure. If you only had shoes, some warm clothing, and you walked at the pace that the guards dictated, you had a decent chance at survival.

"We walked a path of torment, inhuman conditions and sadistic abuse. The guards raced us from one place to another, on land under the control of the Third Reich. The Nazis were so desperate that they could no longer command the tormented multitudes and the commotion that took over. In the disarray of thousands of people, the Nazis beat their humiliating retreat. It was the epilogue of the sweeping drama to eradicate the Jewish race and the Nazi attempt at a Jew-free Europe."

The crowds clogged the roads which were already crowded with Russian prisoners, Polish civilians and German soldiers retreating. Everyone mixed together. Lines of people walking stretched for miles. They marched in the cold of January while beside the road mud puddles gathered and turned red.

Auschwitz' commander Rudolf Hoss, who toured Silesia during the January-February 1945 withdrawal and evacuation, also described the chaos in the roads laden with frightened civilian caravans hauling carts loaded with exhausted children through the snow. In the chaos that prevailed during the withdrawal and escape from the threat of the Red Army, and in light of the major congestion in the roads, Auschwitz' prisoners, who had been an economic asset that the Nazis had counted on to work in their war factories, became a dangerous nuisance.

As the Red Army progressed west, the SS continued to try to march Auschwitz' survivors to work camps in Germany and Austria. "Our march into Nazi Germany shocked us no less than all of the other grave atrocities committed. The unexpected evacuation was an ongoing nightmare. To prevent our release by the Allies, the SS men ran us from one Third Reich-controlled place to another. We were told that we had to be evacuated urgently because when the Russians came, they would execute all of us, prisoners and retreating Germans alike. There were also retreating Wehrmacht military convoys among us. Everyone mixed together. Nonetheless, the Nazis managed to march this human mass, in those impossible conditions, for five months."

The marching convoys also included women who, at the

time of the withdrawal from Auschwitz, were in fairly good health, but the Germans killed many of them along the way. When one of the prisoners collapsed dead, her friends would quickly remove whatever rags they could from her body to warm their own as they marched in the heavy snow.

"Conditions on the road were unbearable. Most of the days that we were on the road, we did not receive food, which exacerbated the constant hunger and fear of dying on the roads in the quickly worsening weather."

The geographical area we passed through was harsh. In elevated regions, and in the Alps, progress was only possible via transport routes that were hard to find. Thousands of prisoners, weak with hunger, encountered topographical barriers on their way. Powerful winds and heavy snow increased their suffering, blocked their way and slowed their progress. The marching commanders wanted to put as much distance as possible between them and the Allied Forces that was closing in on all sides, thus preventing their release.

"For three days, we received no food. We ate weeds,

shrubs, snails, potatoes that civilians had left behind. The death march was an ongoing nightmare that lasted five months, until the Soviet tanks that pulled up ahead of us caught up with our march."

The convoy including Leibl and his four friends was led slowly by train and on foot, and they were only able to move along the main road. "We wanted to sing a little in order to lift the spirits of the elderly and those about to collapse, but our singing was muffled by the incessant shooting of the guards," said Leibl.

Transporting some thirty thousand prisoners on trains turned out to be an impossible task, primarily due to a shortage of rail cars, locomotives, and fuel to run them. Allied aircraft bombings damaged the railways intended to transport military and ammunition for the Wehrmacht units fighting in the area. Anyone for whom there was no space on the train would travel by foot under the close supervision of SS units. But none of the Nazis' desperate acts helped to stop the Allied soldiers.

"One snowy day, we arrived at a rural area. There was a large yard about the size of a football field. There, covered in snow, they sat us down. Each person received two blankets for the night. In the morning we continued walking. Throughout the march we tried not to be seen, to avoid walking in the last row. We always tried to march in the middle of the row as those who lagged behind were shot. Still, two of my friends managed to flee the refugee convoy and escape. They live in Ramat Gan today. A few years ago they asked me to go with them to Poland, but I refused.

"When we arrived at the train station, they gave every one of us a slice of bread and then loaded us onto open train cars in the middle of January. The train took us to Czechoslovakia where we were then marched the entire length of the country on foot. The fierce cold and crowding persisted the entire way. Finally after days of marching they put us onto another train which took us to the outskirts of the camp Mauthausen in Austria. When the train stopped, we got off and began to walk again, guarded by SS men, toward the gates of the camp. The local inmates, who understood the language of the Nazi guards, informed us that the Red Army was approaching from the east and that our release was imminent.

"To our surprise, the camp had showers with hot

water. Slowly and in exemplary orderliness, French, Russian and Polish prisoners were allowed to enjoy a hot shower. To our great surprise, on the third day after our arrival, the Jews among us were also allowed this rare privilege."

German sources reported that in early January 1945, seven hundred thousand prisoners remained in the concentration camps in Germany and Poland. When the camps were liberated, only a quarter million survivors remained. These were those who had survived the death march or were working slave labor in the armament industry and restoring German infrastructure damaged by the Allied bombings. The combination of the American and Soviet attack created 4.5 million refugees.

"After three years as a prisoner of Auschwitz, I left Auschwitz-Birkenau in January 1945 on the 'death march' which terminated for me at the gates of the Mauthausen camp. I barely held on until May sixth, 1945, the day we were liberated from the brutal labor camp by the US Army. If they had come only a few days later, I would have been among the Nazis six million victims," said Leibl.

CHAPTER 11

Work and Extermination Camps — The Mauthausen Camps Complex

At the start of 1942, while the Wehrmacht was heavily invested in its battle in Russia, there was a major shortage of manpower across the Third Reich. So the Nazis recruited hardy prisoners to expand the military industry.

In 1938, a short while after Anschluss — the annexation of Austria to the Third Reich — the Mauthausen camp was established near the city of Lungitz, about 170 kilometers from Vienna. The camp was built as a fortress that looked like a medieval castle and was initially used as a prison for criminals.

Under the harsh command of Commandant Franz

Ziereis, the camp was run very efficiently, as was characteristic of the Nazis. In order to ensure continued military production, Himmler stated on July 10, 1942, that Jewish prisoners would do forced labor in the armament factories throughout the Third Reich and would be held in SS labor camps.

On August 19, 1942, Reinhard Heydrich, Himmler's deputy, categorized the Nazi concentration camps. Mauthausen and Gusen received the most severe classification.

On September 4, 1942, in Berlin, Goebbels presented his view on the need to eliminate the Jews, Gypsies and various prisoners remaining in the extermination camps controlled by the Third Reich, saying, "The idea of elimination through work is the best idea." This statement expressed his view that they could combine mass murder with military production. In his letter to Himmler from September 16, 1942, he expressed it thus, "Jews with the fortitude for work that are headed east will stop their journey so as to do the work of military production." Himmler likewise declared at the end of 1942 that there were no Jews remaining in the territories of the Third Reich except those in the SS work camps.

Above the main entrance to Mauthausen was a bronze statue of a huge eagle with its wings spread and beneath it a large swastika, the emblem of the Third Reich. Throughout the camp was the inscription in enormous letters, "Abandon hope all ye who enter here!" A Russian prisoner later explained to Leibl that this was a quote from Dante's poem *Inferno*.

Leibl and his friends' death march ended in February 1945. With no strength left, a Nazi train spit them out at the entrance to the Mauthausen camp. On foot and guarded by SS men, Leibl Frost, Moshe Brenner, Avraham Berel-Sokal and Lazer Gaskovitz marched toward the camp's gates. Among the transports brought to the camp were also those sent directly from Wysokie. After an initial examination, Leibl and his friends were deemed fit for work.

"Because of our health, we were sometimes scattered among Mauthausen's secondary slave camps. Sometimes the work was manageable but more often it was debilitating and impossible to carry out. But what choice did we have? After all the only other option was our annihilation. We rallied and urged each other on when we had no strength left," Leibl said gravely. "The conditions under which the Jews worked and were kept were infinitely harsher than those of other peoples."

"Extermination through labor," was the principle and the method of the Mauthausen camps. When the prisoners had no strength left after working twelve-hour days in the quarry, or they were too weak or too sick to work, they were sent to the "sick camp" where nobody survived for more than a few days.

The camp spread across 150,000 square meters. During the last two years of its existence, 199,404 prisoners from various European nationalities were put to work: Russians, Poles, Hungarians, Yugoslavs, French, Spanish, Czechs and, of course, Jews. 119,000 of them perished. Of those, 38,120 of the victims were Jews.

Across from the main gate was the plaza where the prisoners had to stand for morning and evening formation. Executions would also be carried out there before all the other prisoners. The prisoners lived in a dense encampment of tents. It was complete chaos and disarray that hastened the death of many. "We lay there on the muddy ground in terribly dense crowding. There was no hygiene whatsoever. No running water, no bathrooms. You had to dig a hole to defecate. Soon mass epidemics of typhus and dysentery broke out, killing many," Leibl described.

Mauthausen and its forty-nine sub-camps was the cruelest slave labor camp in all of World War II. Those labor camps were actually death camps in which they worked the inmates to death, either by exhaustion or the sadistic torture carried out for the entertainment of SS officers. Those prisoners with a diminished capacity for work — due to illness or malnutrition — were killed. Without delay, the Nazis brought in fresh prisoners to take their place. The Third Reich's concept was that when the mining work was over, these prisoners would no longer be needed. They would be taken to the underground tunnels that they themselves had built, and the tunnels would be blown up, killing thousands of them at once.

When the method of killing by torture and forced labor became too expensive or took too long, the Nazis would operate a truck to which a gas chamber was attached. The exhaust pipe extended from the truck and into the chamber which was filled with prisoners that the Nazis no longer had need for. The truck would travel to and from the camp and on its way kill one hundred and twenty prisoners, solving the Nazis' problem of excessive human material.

"There were 186 stairs leading to the mine. After an arduous day of work, the guards would amuse themselves by abusing us, forcing us to carry roughly chiseled chunks of stone, weighing over 50 kilograms, up these 186 stairs. We were ordered to go up all the stairs to the end. These came to be referred to as the "stairs of death." Those who had no strength to climb with their heavy load were shot on the spot by the guards," said Leibl. "All around me I saw inmates collapsing and falling down onto the prisoners behind them. Like dominoes they all toppled down to the bottom. Prisoners who could no longer stand the hard work and malnutrition were consistently dying of exhaustion and hunger. One of the Nazi amusements was to force a prisoner to decide, under threat of death, whether to shoot him or to push the worker in front of him off a ledge," Leibl said with tears in his eyes.

To build the underground factories, the Nazis recruited the Third Reich's best architects and engineers. The emphasis was on planning a system of tunnels deep within the Alps, planning access roads from the main roads to the tunnel entrances, designing railways inside and outside the tunnels, as well as sewage, drainage, electrical, communications, and water supply and ventilation systems. The "cement" project benefited from the best of German planning and efficiency. They invested a great deal of professional work with special, innovative construction methods.

When Allied bombing began to harm the German military industry, the German planners decided to transfer production to underground facilities to protect them from the Allied air raids. The prisoners had to dig several large tunnels into the Alps, under the hills surrounding the camp. They dug to enlarge the underground network of tunnels and hangars in which the Luftwaffe planes were kept. The Germans assembled some 1,250 planes per month there.

Mining in the heat was intolerable and when the temperature dropped below minus thirty degrees centigrade, the rates of death in the mines were especially high. The average prisoner weighed 40 kilograms. The nutritional energy that each of them received daily ranged between 600 to a thousand calories per day. The average life expectancy in the camp started out around six months and fell to three months in 1945. The prisoners were also put to work outside the camp as forced laborers and were exploited in different ways such as working in local farms, setting up fences and archaeological digs. They also built a granite line as an anti-tank barrier.

Melk Labor Camp

"We worked in rotations. After working at Mauthausen, the Nazis transferred us to the Melk labor camp, on the banks of the Danube, about ninety kilometers from Vienna. This was one of Mauthausen's forty-nine sub-camps. The job to be done at Melk was to build an underground arms factory in the heart of the mountain and to dig a tunnel system that would connect between two villages. The main tunnel was three kilometers long. The mountain in which it was built was mostly made of sandstone with a high percentage of the mineral quartz. The sandstone was softer than other types of rocks, so the excavation was accompanied by landslides of sandy soil. As a result, there were endless work accidents in which the many forced laborers perished," Leibl described the project.

Later, the group was assigned to work on projects according to their trades: builders, carpenters, painters, drivers and others. Leibl was not trained in any of those trades, but in order to survive, he offered himself as a proficient carpenter. That was the only way to avoid certain death. "As long as the Nazis found a use for you, your execution would be postponed," he explained.

When Leibl's carpentry project was completed, he, along with a hundred other prisoners, was assigned to unload coal from the tunnels. He and the other prisoners had to move enough of it to run the steam engine of the train that took the workers to the tunnels. The raw material was then taken 7 km by train to one of the biggest weapons factories in Austria.

There were also private factories at Melk — from the largest in German industry, such as the Krupp engine factory which, for some reason, despite using forced labor during the Holocaust, still functions today under its original name.

The barracks that housed the prisoners were terribly overcrowded. The Nazis crammed hundreds of prisoners into barracks designed for ten. Three levels of coarse wooden beds, too small for an adult, were installed for the prisoners. Four people were squashed into each too-narrow bed, and each group of four received just one blanket.

Tens of thousands of prisoners who had come directly from the "death march" produced a terrible bottleneck in the camp. And since the Mauthausen killing machine did not keep pace, the forty-nine sub-camps got fuller and fuller with prisoners living in terrible conditions.

During the twelve months in which the Mauthausen camp operated, thousands of prisoners died. The Nazis invented cruel punishment for any violation. Some of these were to entertain themselves and assuage their boredom. One punishment was twenty lashes of the whip. Another was to not receive the daily meal or to be hung by the feet with one's head down for as long as his punishment had been declared.

There was one solitary barracks in the camp called "the hospital," where SS officer Gottlieb, who was not a doctor, presided. His experiments on patients accounted for the deaths of at least two hundred prisoners. By chance, the "doctor" Gottlieb was recognized in 1960 in the German town of Fulda. He was tried in German court and given a sentence of life imprisonment.

When the Red Army neared the Austrian borders, the SS in the camp began to eradicate the damning evidence, but before they were able to complete the job, the Red Army invaded.

"We were at Melk until March tenth, 1945," Leibl concluded.

Ebensee Concentration Camp

"Like the walking dead, we marched through the camp's main gate," said Leibl. This was a camp with even worse living conditions than Melk. Over 10,000 prisoners met their death at Ebensee, most of them Jews. At its establishment, a third of its inmates were Jews. Later, Gypsies, Russians, Czechs and German and Austrian political prisoners joined them. "The morning after arrival, they shook us awake, shouting 'out!' The Nazis put us into formation and divided the prisoners between the internal sub-camps. At least those of us from the town were not separated from one another. Afterward they gave us coffee and took us outside, naked, into the cold air. We only received clothes after we had been there for several days. The SS dressed us in inmate clothes of thin material and for shoes we had slip-on wooden shoes that quickly fell apart and we were left with no choice but to go barefoot. Each prisoner at Ebensee received 300 grams of bread, a little soup and some coffee. But very soon the Nazis reduced the amount of food and we received only 200 grams of bread. One cannot live on so little, but despite everything, the Nazis cut back even further to just 150 grams per person. Depleted, we worked loading the stones that we mined onto wheelbarrows. On our way we passed by a patch of earth that had grown over with grass. We saw a refreshing, nourishing plant before us. We all fell on the grassy fields, wet with the morning dew. Wildly, we ripped it from the ground and satiated our hunger. Within half an hour, there was not so much as a blade of grass remaining," said Leibl. "I was so tired that I didn't care what they would do next with my broken body. The main thing was to survive this hell. Once, I lay exhausted in a transport, and there was a prisoner dying beside me, holding a piece of bread. He breathed his last breath and, just like on that transport to Auschwitz two years earlier, after I saw that he had died, I took his bread. I was hungry as hell," Leibl admitted.

Ebensee was also a subcamp of Mauthausen. It was built about four kilometers from the town of Ebensee, between Linz and Salzburg, within thick forest. Its purpose was to dig underground tunnels into the hillside for the development of missiles.

Eighty-four steps led to the main tunnel which was 428 meters long and from which 12 side tunnels branched, each one of those 58 meters long. These stairs were similar to the 186 "stairs of death" in Mauthausen, but not as steep. Every 20 stairs there was a short flat space that allowed a few seconds of rest, but these "rest spots" were always occupied by guards who rushed the prisoners and did not allow them to pause. Inmates who lagged behind were shot in the head by the guards. The tunnel digging lasted two years and claimed the lives of thousands of prisoners. Many were executed or died because of the harsh conditions, from hunger, work accidents, and contagious diseases. In the tunnels where the mining work was not yet complete, sand and stone was constantly crumbling over their heads.

"In our despair, many of us ate the bark off trees that grew in the camp. We peeled the husks off the trees with our own hands. They stood there bare," said Leibl. "At Ebensee we realized that the years we had survived at Auschwitz were nothing compared with what awaited us there. We knew that we were not meant to perform regular work. We knew that we would not get out of there before suffering unthinkable abuse. We realized that this place would be crueler than Auschwitz-Birkenau or any other place the Nazis might take our tortured souls throughout the six years of the Holocaust," said Leibl. "While working in quarry, I came down with typhoid, but I hid my illness from the guards, because if the Nazis knew they would have killed me on the spot. Despite my sorry state, I went to work each day. I ate snow until, miraculously, I was cured.

"It became impossible to work while the US Air Force was bombing. Early one morning they brought us to a school where we took shelter. It was a fine day. The view was breathtaking, as though nature did not know what was taking place nearby: there were lakes with clear, fresh water and tall, bushy trees," said Leibl. "In the school there was straw, but we were so tired that it didn't even occur to us to get up and go to the bathroom outside of the space. Everyone urinated wherever he found a spot. The place became filthy and gave off a terrible smell," said Leibl.

"At night, the guards would take us back to work. In order to 'expel the darkness' the Nazis would light lanterns so we could see the American planes bombing endlessly. The skies lit up in the dark of night and the noise of the bombing of the 'freedom jets' sounded like holiday fireworks to us. The Nazis tried to repair a track that had been bombed directly by an American plane, but immediately after they managed to fix it, another American shell bombed it and ripped through it again, this time irreparably. But the Germans did not allow us to rest; the SS brought new tracks and we had to carry them all and lay them in the bombed-out area. Then we had to connect the tracks to one another. All the while we had not eaten a thing. When one of us fell and was killed, we survivors had to carry the extra load of train tracks that he left behind," Leibl explained.

In order to ensure that they would have the required manpower to build the underground arms plant, the "Cement" work camp was established where prisoners paved access roads and laid railroad tracks. To build the tunnels they drilled holes into the Alps, put explosives inside them and then blasted through the hard stone. Then they had to break the rocks further. They crushed and hacked at them, loading the sand that was created onto train cars and pushing them outside through tunnels. Finally they disassembled the wheelbarrows into a pile.

At the start of the job, there were 2,000 prisoners working around the clock in three shifts. After two weeks only some two to three hundred remained, including Leibl and his friends. The rest had been killed in this monstrous work. When Leibl and his friends finished laying the railroad tracks, the Nazis loaded them back onto a train car, without telling them where they were headed.

One day, to their happy surprise, their captors let them shower. This benefit was given in preferential order. First the Germans showered, then the French and others. The Jewish group was the last to enter the showers, but at least they finally showered in hot water. When they left the showers, the Nazis did not give them clothes and they were led back, naked, to their barracks.

"We were at Ebensee until April 1945," concluded Leibl of that brutal period.

Gusen Camp

When Mauthausen filled up beyond capacity with prisoners, the building of a new camp — Gusen — began in Eastern Austria, in the town of Gusen, about 4.5 kilometers from Mauthausen. Like other forced labor camps, Gusen exploited prisoners for hard labor in the granite quarries. The prisoners were also made to work in public corporations, factories and small businesses to benefit the German home front. In 1942, the Mauthausen camps' production was at its peak. Gusen was expanded and provided central storage for the goods and artifacts that had been looted from Jews in the regions conquered by the Third Reich.

It is not known why, despite direct instruction from Heinrich Miller, Gusen prisoners were not killed.

Kommandant Franz Ziereis' plan was to transfer the prisoners quickly to the underground tunnels and factories where they would then bomb the exits. Thankfully, this plan was not carried out.

When Leibl and his friends finished their work at Gusen, the four were brought back to Ebensee. "I was still mining with nine other Jews. I didn't know what was going on outside, so we were surprised to see the Nazis organizing the camp's inmates into formation, divided up according to their hometowns, and sending them out from the camp. We didn't know what the Nazis planned to do with us. From our experience, we expected the worst — our execution. When I saw my friends Abraham Tanenbaum and others standing at the end of their line, I thought they might be taken first for execution, so I suggested that they concentrate into the middle, so that they might be among the last to be evacuated.

"The closer the Allied Forces came, the worse conditions grew for us, but Himmler did not care. On account of crowding and the inability to control masses of people, he had at least 1,000 people shot each day throughout the Mauthausen sub-camps."

The shelling and noise of the Allied aircraft overhead instilled deep fear in the SS guards. On May 3, 1945, the SS guards began to prepare the camp for evacuation. On May 4, the camp Kommandants lost control. The trip to work was stopped and SS men were seen fleeing the camp. Even SS guards fled that day, abandoning the camp and its prisoners to their fate. Guards who realized that their commandant was nowhere to be found decided to escape too. They left their ranks and began to scatter in every direction, walking aimlessly along the road.

"We witnessed the decline of German military discipline. Units disintegrated and spread in all directions. The withdrawal was at its peak. German soldiers who tried to defect were shot, and all of the Germans fled. The area was free of Germans. That was when the prisoners went wild, rioting and looting."

The next morning, two armored American army vehicles entered the camp. The prisoners opened the gates and were released. By May 6, American forces had liberated all of the remaining Mauthausen camps. Most of the SS soldiers were already gone and those that weren't were lynched by camp inmates. Lynching of SS officers took place at the Ebensee camp too.

When Germany surrendered to the Allies, the underground factories were dismantled by the Soviets who sent anything of value to the Soviet Union as spoils of war. In the early summer of 1947, Soviet forces blew up the tunnels.

"I came back via Austria, Czech Republic, Upper Silesia," said Leibl. "I returned to my hometown Wysokie, where I joined the thirty other Jews from the town that had survived the war."

There was an underground immigration network of Jews from Eastern Europe to Central and Southern Europe to smuggle Holocaust survivors to Israel, from 1944-1948. In this mass migration, some 250,000 Eastern European survivors traveled to areas where there were displaced persons camps in Germany, Austria, and Italy.

"I was in Auschwitz for two years, then taken to Mauthausen from January to May 1945, when I was liberated by the American army. On November second, 1942, I was deported from my town. I returned three years and two days later, on August 1, 1945. Almost no Jews remained in Wysokie's neighboring towns. When I first set foot in Wysokie, I saw the extent of the damage. I went to the place where my home had once stood, where my little brothers played, and their families had lived. I also met the Gentile who had led me to the death camps back then. I didn't have the strength to bear a grudge. Out of my family which had numbered ten people, I alone remained. My friends Moshe Brenner, Avraham Berel-Sokal and Lazar Gaskovitz also survived the Holocaust. If the Allied Forces had come any later, I too would have been among the Nazi's six million victims.

"After liberation in 1945, when I reached the train station nearest Wysokie, I was told that my friend Pesach Segal, whose father was very rich and had been shot in the mouth by the Germans, had survived. I went to him and he gladly took me in. I was like a family member in his home. Pesach and his wife, another Wysokie native, had hidden among Gentiles and so were saved. After the war Wysokie was almost entirely '*judenrein*' — free of Jews. Everything was destroyed.

"In 1946, with the help of HaBricha movement, I left Poland. I went to Silesia, where groups of Jews from Russia arrived from the camps and all over. We gathered there and then traveled to Israel. We traveled through Czechoslovakia to Austria and from there, via Italy to the shores of Israel. I was among those immigrants of the illegal immigrant ship *Exodus*, upon which we were deported to Cyprus by the British Mandate in November 1947.

"Finally I arrived in Israel with other immigrants before its independence in 1948. Right away I joined the Haganah organization. With the establishment of the state, I enlisted to the military. I fought in the Galilee during the War of Independence. After our victory, I moved to Kibbutz Ga'ash, where I made my home."

CHAPTER 12

A Visit to Wysokie

In December 1991, Lech Walesa, a shipyard man from Gdansk (who later became the Polish president), led the Solidarity trade union. His movement, which was joined by countless supporters, eventually overthrew the Communist regime's monopoly and led to its dramatic disintegration — the collapse of the Soviet Empire. The whole world watched as the gates of the Soviet empire opened to the Western world. Thus I was given the opportunity to visit the place where my family's roots lie.

In October 1992, I boarded a plane in New York (where I was living at the time) run by the Polish LOT airline. Seven hours later, I landed in Warsaw. In the taxi in which I made my way to the capital, I saw Poland before me, as it had been left by the Nazis in 1945 and handed over to the Soviet Union. Communism had taken over everything. There were poor neighborhoods on either side of the road whose buildings still bore scars and holes from the gunshots of the German Wehrmacht. On the outskirts of Warsaw, I was stunned by the remains of elegant buildings designed in the fashion of historical architecture - an offshoot of Soviet culture. Monuments and sculptures that had been the heart of Polish culture were desecrated. A huge gate — Stalin's gift to the Polish nation — still stood intact downtown. The Poles who had suffered for forty-four years under that Soviet tyrant didn't dare get rid of the monument that reminded them of their dark past.

A dark, gloomy atmosphere welcomed me to the capital that I had visited many times as a child. I stayed in the Polish flagship hotel Novotel and went to walk around Jerusalemska Ulica (Jerusalem street) which had survived the Nazis' ruinous war. It looked like the street had been frozen in time, as though it were abandoned in 1945. The smell of cheap cigarette smoke and fumes of vodka rose from the sad-looking cafes. Cars and buses emitted poisonous smoke that the pedestrians inhaled. People were hidden within their layers of warm clothing - black leather jackets that had seen better days stained the streets with their gloom. Faces looked long and depressed. Drunk men stumbled through the street. Although Communism was behind them, the Poles could not expel it from their souls. Unsmiling people gave short, indifferent answers when I asked them for directions in my broken Polish.

At the train station, where I waited a long time for the train that would take me the three-hour ride to the town of Wysokie Mazowickie, passengers were seated at cafes with plastic cups smoking and gnawing on pork sausage sandwiches, as they sipped cheap vodka. Empty cigarette packets and alcohol bottles were scattered all over the station floor. There were no staff at the station to help me and I was "stuck" with two heavy suitcases that I had to carry through the winding underground tunnels to the platform. A Polish man saw me struggling and offered his services. He carried my suitcases up until the train platform. I paid him and thanked him for his generosity. The train was very late to depart. As we passed by villages, I envisioned convoys of Jews being led to a train station that would take them to their demise. In my imagination, I saw the Gentiles standing by the roadside calling out to the victims, "the Nazis will make soap from your bodies."

The train passed through many kilometers of greenery. It was a cultivated land of agricultural villages endowed with rain and fertile soil. On its way the train passed by an abandoned area, some ten kilometers long. There were piles of ash laying around and burned remains were scattered throughout. It was evident that this was an abandoned Nazi extermination camp. I was amazed by how surreal it was to see it. Suddenly I spotted a tombstone in memory of those who had perished in the camp. It was built from 17,000 stones on which the victims' names were engraved. It looked like a Jewish cemetery. From afar I saw a sign bearing the name "Treblinka". I remembered my mother telling me that the Jewish doctor and writer Janusz Korczak had been a prisoner here. From her stories I recalled that the camp was about 30 kilometers from our town and many of our townspeople were brought here to die.

I got off the train at the Bialystok station, in North Eastern Poland, bordering Lithuania and some 30 km from Wysokie. From there I boarded a train that would take me to the town where I was born. Along the way

I saw more drunks, almost stumbling into the roads, endangering their lives as well as those of the drivers.

I got off at my station. A sign placed at the entrance to the town bore its name "Wysokie Mazowickie". My heart beat fast. My head was spinning, my heart jittery. I couldn't believe my eyes: was it possible that here I was, standing before the entrance to the town in which I was born? In which many members of my family were killed. In which my parents hid from the Nazis. I wandered its unpaved streets. There were still holes streets from Nazi shelling. This was my first day and the town looked as though it had been abandoned by its residents. I turned to a farmer who was leading a cow on a rope and in my meager Polish I asked him the way to the Jewish cemetery. The farmer smiled, revealing gaps in his mouth where teeth were missing. "You're standing on it," he replied. It appeared as though nobody had stood on this spot for many years. I was met with thick, thorny bushes. I made my way through them, and they scratched my arms as I bent their prickly branches aside to see the land I was standing on. Suddenly I saw the remains of tombstones, brutally mutilated. I asked the Gentile who had desecrated the graves. "The Nazis," he replied. "They used the marble stones that covered the graves to pave sidewalks." I remembered my mother's stories in which the Nazis forced the Jews to break their own parents' gravestones then denied them the right to so much as walk upon them. They could only walk on unpaved trails. Furious, my heart stood still as I entered the church where the townspeople said their prayers. A nun saw my face and asked me who I am. I told her that I was born in this town and I asked her for the address of Kroll Bialitsky — the Gentile who gave refuge to my grandfather, Shmuel Izak, my mother and her sisters Basha and Chaya. "Get into my car," she said. "Bialitsky, that's Hemi, I'll take you to him." Within minutes we were at his door. "Rivka!" he said in amazement, looking emotional. "No I am not Rivka but her daughter, Sarah," I replied. I knew that I looked like my mother, so much so that he thought I was her. I was so moved that he called over his whole family to come and see the "miracle." Within ten minutes his wife and daughters had laid the table full of the best of Polish cuisine. There were *shinka, buchek,* sausages of various cuts of pork, hot potato pancakes, salted fish and many other delicacies. He told me that he had been a childhood friend and in the same class as my father. He described how his father had hidden members of my mother's family along with other Jews in the attic of his home. He asked me if I wanted to see it. "Yes," I said excitedly. We walked a hundred meters until we reached an old house made of earth which stood empty of inhabitants. It was like an illusion. The house was dark. The Gentile led me up the shaky steps which ended in an attic. "Here," he said. "I hid your family and some other townspeople." I couldn't believe my eyes. The place was too small to fit ten refugees.

We left to tour the town. Bialitsky led me to the town's main plaza - *rynek* in Polish. This was where the old market had been. This was the town's past lifeline of trade had stood. Here, Jews and Gentiles alike laid out their wares. But as I stood in this center which used to be full and bustling, I saw only chickens pecking at crumbs and remains. The place was abandoned and neglected.

Bialitsky pointed to a long, two-story building. "This building used to belong to your grandfather, your mother's father — Shmuel Izak, who owned a lot of property in the town. These days," he went on, "the building serves as the town's city hall." He pointed to a sign hung on the building which said: "Built in 1937."

From there he took me in his car outside the city where

an old, abandoned house stood roofless and windowless. It looked like the place had known better, grander days. This had been the estate of my father's family, the Segals. This was where the Nazis had invaded in 1941 and turned it into their headquarters. He pointed to an empty yard just beside the house, about an acre in size. This was where my father's family mill stood. The mill had provided flour for all the surrounding towns and electrical power to the entire region. He pointed to a rusted sign on the ground that bore the words "Segal Meizner Flour Mill." Meizner was my father's cousin and a partner in the family business. To this day I still have a photograph of that sign.

Bialitsky was not considered especially merciful since my family essentially bought their lives from the Gentile for a great sum of money and the assets that they transferred to him.

With a heavy heart I got onto a bus that would take me back to Bialystok. There I waited a few hours until the train came, which took me back to Warsaw.

In Warsaw, my sister Rachela joined me. She had come from Israel to share this traumatic experience of revisiting our roots. We rented a car and driver who would take us all over Poland for a week. The value of the local currency - the Polish zloty, was so low that when converted to the American dollar it was unbelievably cheap. The driver took us to Wrozlaw, where my family had passed through in August 1946, after liberation on their way back to Wysokie. In 1945, at the end of the war, when my parents returned from "hell" to Wysokie, the Gentiles were cruel and prevented them from returning to their ruined houses, from repairing and reestablishing their lives anew. Those same Gentiles, who had been employed by my family's flour mill before the war, and had wide-spread business relations before the Holocaust, then organized against them when they returned home. Life in the town was dangerous and impossible. In mid-1946, when I was just six months old, my family moved to the magnificent Polish city of Wroclaw. There, in June 1948, my sister Rachela was born. Wroclaw is in southwestern Poland, bordering Germany. In fact it had once been part of German territory. With the defeat of the Nazis, it was unilaterally annexed by Poland in 1945. Our family lived there until May 1950 when we boarded the rickety Greek ship which took us to the then two-year-old State of Israel.

We toured the pretty city, which is today the fourth largest in Poland. From the many bridges over the Oder River, connect between the small islands of the city, we viewed the town, wandered the main square and its great cathedral, walked the colorful market. Tired, we returned each night to our hotel.

In the hotel lobby, something interesting transpired. Buses packed with German tourists, all of them my parents age, came and spilled out into the city. Before the second world war, these people had been residents of this city. In 1944, with its annexation to Poland, its German residents abandoned it and went to live in Germany. Now they were back for a roots trip, and I looked in the eyes of every one of them who passed me by, asking with my eyes, "How many Jews did you kill?" If only I could have spat a few words in their faces. Although I consider myself a liberal person, I could never look a German my father's age in the eyes without an accusatory gaze. Former Israeli Prime Minister, Menachem Begin, may his memory be blessed, used to say, "The German drinks anti-Semitism at his mother's breast."

This was Sunday and the city didn't have much entertainment to offer. The Germans began to get on their buses for a tour of the surrounding lakes and rivers. The bus driver offered us to join their trip out of town. My short-tempered sister wanted to join them. I refused, but when she insisted, I agreed on the condition that she promise she wouldn't tell them that we were Jews from Israel. The other passengers looked at us, wondering what these two women were doing on their bus. With the little Polish I knew I explained that the tour guide had invited us to join. The "roots from the past" tourists spoke German, but I quickly understood the topic of their conversation. Not much time passed before they began to talk about us and refer to us as "shvartzas." At this point Rachela couldn't keep her promise and in broken Polish she reprimanded them and told them precisely what she thought of them. The atmosphere on the bus was tense. When we arrived at the first tourist site, we parted ways from the others, but we returned and got back on the bus eventually to return to the city with them. We had no choice; the city streets that Sunday were silent, and we had no other way to get back to the hotel.

CHAPTER 13

The Ship That Wasn't Meant to Sail

A huge wave accompanied by thunder and lightning suddenly swept the deck and nearly took me along with it. Trapped in the stream of water, I gripped the rickety railing to regain balance. I stuck my head out of the whirling waters, desperate for some air, and another wave blasted through and filled my mouth with salt water.

"Help me, I'm drowning," a woman's voice came through the waves, "Good God! Why did you save me from Hitler just to drown me now in the depths of the Mediterranean?"

The woman, her wet dress tight against her thin, quivering body, thrust out her arms and legs in a desperate attempt to grab onto the life raft. All at once she was swept away and a huge wave spat her out onto the deck where she was tended by the ship's crew. Around me, passengers floated on the water that flooded the ship while the sailors scrambled to pull them out.

"Mom, Dad, someone!" I cried in desperation. In that chaos, I felt like even if I were to be saved, I would remain alone in this cruel world. Bitter tears streamed down my cheeks and were swallowed up by the surging waters. Exhausted, I gripped the lifebuoy that the ship's crew threw toward the passengers. I tried to paddle toward our cabin somewhere in the belly of the ship, but water poured out into all the passageways and thwarted my attempts. Suddenly I felt a strong hand grab my arms and pull me to them. "Sit here, don't move until I find your parents," the unknown man instructed.

At the start of that journey, I was four years old; who listens to a young child whose place is among her toys and dolls? On the one hand, I was too young to understand the hardships that my parents had suffered during the war years, and on the other hand, I realized that my young life had been loaded onto that dilapidated Greek ship. I wondered if the new house that we were sailing toward would be sturdier than this boat, and if it would be like the house we had left behind.

The house in which I had grown up until that point was surrounded by a well-tended garden, in a prestigious neighborhood of Wroclaw, Poland. My dreams carried me to the kinds of palaces in which Cinderella awaited her beloved. Kings and noblemen lived there. Their refined lives are written about in the book, *The Magical Prince*.

I missed the elegant tavernas in Wroclaw's green gardens where, on Sundays in the evening hours, my parents and other coupled friends of theirs would dance Israeli dances, while I watched them, eating an ice cream cone sprinkled with chocolate sprinkles. Tears sprung to my eyes as I remembered that I would never again skate on the frozen Vistula River, while my Uncle Haim held my hand, never releasing me from his grip. I would glide from him toward the thinner spots that could not have borne the weight of a grown man. Uncle Haim got mad at me and told me to come back immediately, but I enjoyed scaring and teasing him. Even though I was punished for doing so more than once, I always repeated the prank.

But our voyage was nothing like the luxurious sailing vacation on the Vistula River of the previous summer. By now, most of my toys were wet, soaked, sunken somewhere in the depths of the Mediterranean.

Mom came to get me from the corner where the stranger had sat me down and wrapped her arms around me. I snuggled into her warmth and her pleasant smell that even the sea had not managed to overpower. I felt the sense of security that I always felt in her presence. "Don't worry, child, it's always a bit stormy this time of year but you'll love paddling in the Mediterranean in the summer," she promised. But I vowed not to dip so much as my fingers in these stormy waters.

Toward evening the sea calmed down and the passengers hung their clothes to dry in the spring wind. The ship's crew plugged up the hole they had found in its hull, and the *Anatolia* sailed on its way, with a blue and white flag flying from its mast. It took God seven days and seven nights to create the world, and the same amount of time for the *Anatolia* to bring us to our new world.

On May 15, 1950, the ship anchored in the Haifa port. Despite our exhaustion, we marveled at the beauty of the city of Haifa from the deck of the ship, the gateway to the two-year-old State of Israel. Mount Carmel stood in all its glory and at its feet the sea lapped at the golden sand. At the far end of the port, those arriving united with their families welcoming them with tears of happiness; until then nobody knew who had survived the Nazi inferno.

Dad carried me to the pier and down the ladder that dangled from the deck. Mom descended after him, holding my two-year-old sister Rachela in her arms. It was so good to finally stand on solid ground. There was no family waiting for us since most of them had perished in the Holocaust. Those who had survived the war had emigrated from the displaced persons camp in Germany — a transit camp for refugees of the camps — where they were detained after liberation from the ghettos and extermination camps until they were dispatched by the Allied soldiers to their respective regions. My grandfather, Shmuel Izak, then made his way along with my Uncle Hezkel to the United States, while another aunt, Dverka, emigrated to Australia with her husband. My parents refused to accompany them to any other Diaspora than Poland. They were determined not to live any longer in exile but to immigrate to the new State of Israel.

Our immigration was traumatic. At age four, it was already hard for me to understand how my parents were willing to give up our happy, comfortable life, to move to a world I could never have imagined would be so different. I resented being "kidnapped" from my indulgent childhood without justification. "We will not exchange Polish Diaspora for American Diaspora," they said.

The passengers descended one after the other from the dangling ladder. Soon the immigrants and those who came to greet them were all jumbled together. People fell upon one another's shoulders until it was impossible to tell who had just arrived and who had come to meet them. Immigrants gathered their belongings, thanking God and kissing the ground of the Holy Land. My parents did not stoop for God.

Mom wore her blue cashmere sweater, a little warm for the humid spring day. Her almond eyes glittered with happiness. Her anticipation and longing for this day had given her the strength to survive the years of the Holocaust. Suddenly young, tanned men gathered around us, greeting us with wide smiles, dressed in khaki shorts and bucket hats that shielded their faces from the blazing sun. "Pioneers," they were called. Following a series of bureaucratic tasks, government officials signed our passports and made us Israeli citizens. The number

42474957 was now a part of my identity. Rachela got the subsequent number.

A truck smeared with mud and dust, which looked like it had just returned from the battlefield, stood ready for us new immigrants. Dad handed me over into the arms of a pioneer who stood on the truck. Mom likewise handed the baby, wrapped in a pink blanket, into the arms of another pioneer. Dad hopped into the truck bed and held out his hand to Mom who was careful not to expose what was hidden under her dress. The truck began to drive.

"Where are they taking us?" I sobbed.

"Soon we'll get to the Pardes Hanna transit camp," Mom tried to comfort me. "We will live there for some time until we find a permanent place," she promised.

I was quiet. How could I resist a place whose exotic name I had never even heard before?

Lakes of green water alongside the road gave off a stench which rose through the warm air. "What are these puddles?" I asked.

"Those aren't puddles!" said Mom. "Those are the swamps I told you about, that the pioneers have been working so hard to dry out."

"They're green," I observed.

"Don't get near them," Mom ordered hastily. "They can give you malaria which can be fatal."

I didn't bother to ask what malaria was since I had no intention of wading into those murky waters.

"Do you see those tall trees? Those are eucalyptus trees. They were brought here from Australia to dry out the swamps."

I was not at all impressed by their contribution.

The truck turned East toward a dirt road, an unpaved, bumpy and dusty not-quite-road. I grit my teeth. Even the shaking of the ship had not shocked my innards as much. The air was sticky, and our bodies were hit by a wave of heat. My delicate hands were blackened like coal and my nostrils filled with sand. "There aren't even any houses here, it's all empty and ugly," I protested again. Nobody responded. Along the side of the road were abandoned military camps. "Those are the British army bases," Dad explained.

"So where are all the soldiers?" I asked.

"I'll tell you when you're older," he said dismissively. I thought to myself that he would have a great many things to explain to me when I was older and went on observing the view which did not interest me.

Endless orchards of citrus trees laden with fruit hanging from them like colorful balloons lifted my spirits somewhat. A smiling pioneer threw a juicy orange in my direction, a rare and expensive fruit in Poland. I only got to taste it when I had the flu, when Mom bought me oranges and clementines. "You need calcium," she would say.

The sweet fruit calmed me a little. I leaned back against the cool tarpaulin of the truck and comforted myself with memories of the recent past. In my mind I sailed back to Poland, to our big house in Wroclaw. The living room was scattered with trunks and suitcases which would soon be closed, waiting to be loaded onto the train that would take us to Venice, where we would board the ship *Anatolia*. I was sorry to leave my toys behind.

"You're allowed to take one doll," Mom declared. That was a hard decision which I faced along with my friend Elka whose family was also about to make the trip with us to Israel. The decision came down to our similar dolls Lula and Ella, whose heads were crowned with golden curls. When we spanked them lightly their light blue eyes closed, and their lips opened and let out a sweet sob that pleased me. We decided that even though the dolls looked like two Polish Gentile girls, they would still be permitted to emigrate, with us, to Israel.

"What will we do with the other dolls?" Elka asked me. Not a moment passed before I came up with a good solution. "Well, we don't want the dolls to fall into the hands of non-Jewish girls," I said. Elka nodded her head in agreement. We stood beside the wood stove. I held my oldest, nameless doll, by her arm and leg. We smashed their curl-free heads on the floor of the room and when we finished crushing my doll's skull, we took care of Elka's. After that we put the rejected dolls into the burning fireplace. A harsh smell of burning filled the air. Dad cried out at the sight and delivered several blows to our bottoms. As punishment, we were denied the right to bring even one beloved doll to Israel.

As I daydreamed, leaning my head against the tarp of the truck, the memory of that loss returned to again and frustrated me. I turned to look out at the landscape which only increased my anger. After the dusty one-hour drive, the truck stopped with a great deal of noise and a cloud of dust.

"Where are we?" I cried.

"We've arrived at the Pardes Hanna transit camp," Dad declared.

We were greeted by a gray jungle of tents scattered among the dunes. Joylessly, I got down from the truck, straight into the arms of another Jewish Agency official who also represented the state. He was thin and held a board under his arm which bore a list of immigrants. His head was bowed as he strained his eyes to read our names, and he located the list of our family members. My two-year-old sister was not ready for these impossible conditions and burst into bitter tears in my mother's arms. I popped her milk bottle into her mouth. Luckily for us, the liquid hadn't soured in this oppressive heat and she drank from it eagerly. We were led to a tent who loose fabric waved hello in the warm wind. Tired and disappointed, my little body sweaty, I looked around fearfully. In desperation, I threw myself on the bed, the only piece of furniture in our new home, and exhausted myself crying until I fell into a troubled sleep.

A spray of warm white liquid splashed on my arms and bare feet, waking me from my sleep. A man and woman dressed in white, as though they were doctors or nurses, stood beside me spraying me with the loathsome liquid.

I opened my eyes in shock and cried out to my father, "Tell them to stop!"

"Don't worry, Sarah," he tried to calm me. "They're spraying us with DDT just to disinfect us from the germs that we may have picked up in the unsanitary conditions on the ship."

I ran off and made my way between the tents where the other immigrants gave in to being sprayed. There was a great commotion all around me and many of the newly arrived expressed their dissatisfaction with the inadequate conditions. Insulted and enraged they protested before the embarrassed officials from the Jewish Agency. I got lost and couldn't find my way back to our tent. The people all around spoke in a mix of languages that I did not understand. I felt foreign and alienated, afraid to lose my mother, father and little sister. I did what I could — I cried. Suddenly a pleasant, smiling woman approached me. "Can I help you?" she asked me in Polish, the one language I could understand. She held my hand and led me to our tent.

"I want to go home," I wailed. "Back to our house in Wroclaw. If you all insist on living here, let me go home," I demanded.

"Where will you live alone in Wroclaw?" asked Dad.

"I'll go live with my nanny, Broncha (who had remained in Poland). Why didn't you bring her with us?" I raged.

"Broncha isn't Jewish and her home is not in Israel. We finally arrived in a land where everyone is Jewish," replied my father. "Besides, you never really liked her," he teased. "You always called her the green monkey."

I was silent.

Most days at the transit camp I met dozens of children whose fate was like mine. Together we wandered aimlessly around the encampment of tents. Thorns and weeds scratched my bare legs and arms, in this "Garden of Eden" of snakes. When I discovered the prickly pear cactus bush, rich with sweet orange fruits, I reached out to pick one. I was instantly pricked with many tiny, fine thorns. The more Mom tried to pull them from me, the more they scratched my arms, tongue and throat.

Later, one of the other children brought an empty can, tied it to a stick, held it out to the thorny bushes and used it to pick the juicy fruit. We rolled the sabras fruit in the sand, peeled them off and now we could enjoy the fruit without worry. I later learned that children born in Israel were nicknamed "Sabar," the Hebrew word for prickly pears because they were thick skinned and prickly on the outside but soft and sweet on the inside.

At night, the foxes howled. The winter of 1950 was considered one of the harshest winters the young country had had, the winds blew violently into the tents and shook us from our sleep. The down blanket that had survived the storm at sea and kept me warm as a child could not protect me against the cold. Fierce rains tore at the pathetic roof over our heads and our feet sunk in sticky, boggy mud.

One night I woke up from my sleep. "Mama, I need to go to the bathroom," I said.

"Number one or number two?" Mom asked.

"Number two," I answered. If it had been a number one, I could have taken care of it in the shadows of one of the tents. With the help of a flashlight, Mom led me a few hundred meters away. There stood a big tent, one that reminded me of the circus tents that had sometimes come to our Polish town. It was the communal bathroom. Among the cells, divided up by tarp into private stalls, we saw a hole that was already overflowing with 'number twos' from the guts of other immigrants.

"Mom! I'm afraid I'll fall inside! Hold my hand!" Mom held my arm. I leaned over the hole and when I'd finished, before I could straighten my pajamas, a siren was heard from a truck coming toward us. There was a big black tank on the truck, the kind of tanks I had seen earlier touring the transit camp carrying oil. This time a thick black tube was being dragged from the heart of the truck. One of the pioneers held the pipe and approached the tent in which some of the immigrants were still taking their time. I panicked and started to run away. Mom chased after me and explained that I didn't need to fear that truck, that it was the sewage truck and it had come to drain and clean up the "kaka" of the new immigrants.

Tears of fear and bitterness put me quickly back to sleep. I saw Wroclaw before my eyes. On a winter night, covered in deep, gray snow, the streets were deserted. I walked, shaking from cold, along Jerusalemska Ulica, the main street, which was always busy and colorful. Fear came over me. I didn't know how I'd gotten to this place on my own. I knocked on locked doors, but the residents drove me away. Nobody came to my aid. My boots sunk in the snow and froze my toes. I lost my way and kept walking without knowing where. Suddenly I heard the shrill sound of a siren, similar to that of the sewage truck, except that this time no friendly Israeli pioneers jumped out, but rather three soldiers dressed in brown uniforms and a red swastika on their shirtsleeves. They looked cruel, like those that my mother had told me about, that always wanted to kill her. I knew that unlike her, I wouldn't be able to escape them. I gathered my strength and began to run until I was short of breath. I sunk deeper and deeper into the puddles that the melting snow had left behind. The soldiers followed me, shooting in my direction, but they didn't catch me. Despairing, with no chance of getting away, I saw a sewer gaping before me without a lid. Without hesitation, I jumped into it and my body sunk into the human excrement at its bottom. With my frozen, painful hands, I pulled the concrete lid, placed just beside the pit, over my head. I didn't cry, I knew that I had to be strong, because if not — I would fall into the hands of the Nazis, as so many Jews had. One of the brown soldiers lifted the concrete lid above me and shouted into the hole, "Out, you stinking little Jew!" I pleaded with him, "Please, leave me be, I didn't do anything wrong," but he must not have understood Polish, and he pushed my head under the filthy waters of Wroclaw with his hard, black boot.

I shouted in fear and opened my eyes. I saw Mom and Dad leaning over me, stroking my head and trying to calm me. I told them my dream. Mom was worried and Dad was angry. "Why do you fill her head with the horror stories that you went through? Why not save her the tragedy that she is anyway still too young to understand? You could also do to relax a little, because those thoughts give you attacks of mania that you are helpless against." Mom was offended. She crouched in her corner of the tent and cried. I called for her to help.

"It's not Mom's fault. I was afraid that if I went back to the bathroom tent I would fall inside. Like in Ka-Tzetnik's book that you read to me when I couldn't sleep, when you told me about the horrors you experienced in the Holocaust. When can we leave this terrible place?"

"Soon," Dad replied. I despised that word more than any other. I knew that my parents weren't planning to leave anytime soon. After all, since we'd left our home in Poland, we didn't have anywhere else to go.

After the summer, the transit camp's nursery school opened up. I was surrounded by children who looked and dressed differently than me. None of them approached me, everyone stuck to the kids that looked like them. My sister, who was two, was the only one I could confide my troubles to. Slowly but surely I learned Hebrew and refused to speak my mother tongue with my parents. I did everything I could not to look like a little refugee girl, a new immigrant like the others. I no longer wore my taffeta dresses; instead, I wore blue cotton pants, tight against my long, skinny hips from which protruded my matchstick legs.

Life in the transit camp was intolerable. Over and over again I asked my parents, "When will we leave this place?" And the answer was always, "Soon."

We were among the mass immigration of Holocaust survivors from Europe. In the 1950s, there were 129 transit camps all over the country which housed jobless immigrants from Europe and the Arab world. In order that the new immigrants not lose their minds idling, the country created public works projects for the unemployed. Dad worked such jobs weeding on the nearby kibbutzim, while Uncle Haim was recruited to the Israel Defense Force.

After eight months in the transit camp, a change came. We were transferred to a long white block which was divided into sections without partitions or walls in between them. It was a building which in the past had served as British soldiers' living quarters, and now it had been assigned to us new immigrants. Without walls for privacy, we were deprived of any modesty. Mom hung starched white sheets between us and our neighbors: the Polish family to the right and the Yemenite family on the left. We cooked our food on paraffin which left its aftertaste on everything. I missed Mom's golumpki (stuffed cabbage) and the crimson-colored borscht with high-fat cream.

In the dense conditions in which we were living, the Poles learned to hate the Romanians and the Iraqis came to hate the Yemenites. The immigrants sank into the hateful discrimination that they had tried to leave behind in the Diaspora.

A short while later we became aware that someone was visiting, someone with immaculate Hebrew who was not dressed like the others but in a tailored suit. My parents were very surprised to see him and fell upon him, crying and laughing all at once. He was a close family friend who had even studied in the yeshiva with my father in Wysokie Mazowickie, where I was born. His name was Slovik, and when he came to Israel as a pioneer, he changed his name to the Hebrew "Zamir". Tzvi Zamir was the head of the Magdiel settlement council in the Sharon region. Just like that, within a few days, my parents once again loaded up our belongings onto a truck. This time, we were going to live in the house that the head of Magdiel had arranged for us. By the age of five, I had learned that connections are everything.

CHAPTER 14

Where Will I Go? To Whom Can I Turn?

According to Leibl, there was an active movement was active in Europe between the years 1944 to 1948 — an underground Jewish emigration which brought Holocaust survivors from Eastern Europe together and brought them to Central and Southern Europe. Displaced persons camps were set up for them in Germany, Austria and Italy, and they stayed there until they received visas to immigrate to the United States, Australia and other countries. Some of the refugees also managed, with great difficulty, to reach Israel — still Palestine at that time. In that mass immigration, nearly 250,000 Holocaust survivors traveled to Israel.

"In 1945, via Austria, Czechoslovakia and Upper Silesia, on a journey by foot and train I returned to Wysokie, the town where I was born," told Leibl. "When I arrived at the train station nearest Wysokie, I was told that my friends Pesach Segal and his brother Haim, whose father was very wealthy and who had been shot in the mouth by the Germans, survived. I walked to their house, which had survived the Wehrmacht shelling, and they greeted me warmly. I was like a member of the family in their home. Pesach and his wife Rivka, who was also a native of our hometown, had survived by hiding in gentile homes throughout the war."

"For two years I suffered all of the tortures of Auschwitz," said Leibl. "On November second, 1942, I was deported from my town. In January 1945, after a cruel death march, I was taken to the Mauthausen camp and on May seventh, 1945, I was liberated by the American army. I returned to Wysokie three years and two days later. Out of the 2,500 Jews who had lived in our town before the Holocaust, I returned to find only thirty survivors. The surrounding towns had almost no Jews left at all. As I first entered Wysokie, I saw the extent of its damage. I went up to where my house had once stood, the place where my little brothers had played, the place where my older brothers and their families had lived. Everything was in ruins. I met the Gentile who, in 1942, had led me to the train that would take me to the death camp. I was too exhausted to take revenge. From among my ten family members, I was the only one left. If the Allied armies had taken any longer to arrive, I too would have been among the Nazis' six million victims."

"In 1946, with the help of the HaBricha movement, I left Poland and went to Silesia. I traveled via Czechoslovakia, through Austria, where groups of displaced Jews came from Russia, from the extermination camps and all around. There we gathered and waited for a permit to immigrate to Palestine, which was soon to become Israel."

CHAPTER 15

The British Mandate

Israel, previously known as Palestine, had been periodically invaded by different colonial powers for thousands of years. Sacred to Jews, Moslems, and Christians, the region was torn apart, each nation claiming its historically exclusive rights to continuous existence in the area. The Roman and Iranian empires—among the Turkish Ottoman Empire - from the 13th to the 20th century. They annihilated the Jewish population or exiled them to their Diasporas throughout the world. But for more than two thousand years, the Jews never stopped working and praying for return to their homeland. Every prayer they concluded with the words, "For the next year in Jerusalem."

Great Britain was the last empire to rule Palestine (1922 until 1948). Britain was empowered by the League of

Nations, the body that preceded the United Nations. The League of Nations recognized the historical connection of the Jewish nation to Palestine and so did the British Queen. Britain was entrusted "to see to the well-being of the Jewish-Arabic population in Palestine." They were supposed to ensure the establishment of a Jewish national homeland in Palestine, also known as Eretz Israel, the Land of Israel. However, the British Mandate never lived up to what was expected and abused the power entrusted to them.

Britain tried not to challenge the fragile balance between the Arab and Jewish populations in their dominion. They were afraid the Jewish Aliyah – immigration, this "foreign invasion," would weaken the British control over Palestine. On May 17 the British government published its White Paper of 1939 stating that within ten years an independent Arab state with a Jewish minority population would be established in Palestine. In five years, accordingly, Jewish immigration to Palestine would be terminated. Until then, they allowed only seventy-five thousand Jewish immigrants per year to enter the country. This document also forbade Jews to acquire more than 5% of land in Eretz Israel and restricted settlements. The white paper will be forever a disgrace and shame for the United Kingdom. Had this government allowed entrance to Jews who tried to escape Europe on the eve of World War II, numerous lives could have been saved.

At that time, Hitler was gaining power in Germany and his plan to annihilate the Jewish nation, so definitively set forth in his *Mein Kampf*, was very well known. However, it did not make the British reconsider their decision.

The British limited quota for Olim- new immigrants, did not discourage young Jews from fleeing anti-Semitic Europe and seeking shelter in Palestine. The daring, brave pioneers, who made the dangerous voyages between 1922 and 1948, were called "Maapilim." They found creative ways to penetrate the British blockade. Illegal immigration was their only solution, so they organized a number of unauthorized sea passages. Many Maapilim perished on voyages or were arrested by British authorities while attempting to enter Eretz Israel. Only a few of these operations managed to break through the British blockade and bring their passengers ashore. During the 26 years of British Mandate, about 125,000 Maapilim reached the shores of Haifa and Tel Aviv. It was a symbol of the Jewish struggle to return to their homeland from the longest Diaspora.

EXODUS 1947

In 1946, with the help of HaBricha (the Jewish escape movement), Leibl left Poland. He joined other Jewish survivor-refugees that gathered from all parts of Europe and boarded the SS *Exodus 1947*.

The crowded vessel *Exodus 1947* sailed from a small port near Marseilles, France in July of that year with 4,554 Holocaust survivors aboard (Leibl was one of them). As soon as it left the waters of France, British destroyers shadowed over it. When they were about thirty-five kilometers from the port of Haifa, the British soldiers stopped it and boarded the boat. The Maapilim desperately tried to defend themselves with empty food cans and other rudimentary weapons. Four Maapilim were killed and the ship was severely damaged. The British towed the *Exodus* to Haifa where it was repaired, the passengers imprisoned on it and the ship returned to France.

Terrorized and agonized at the thought of being returned to the countries in which they barely escaped execution, they decided to strike for their freedom. When the ship arrived back in Marseilles, the rebellious passengers refused to disembark. They remained on the *Exodus* for 24 days, holding out for their right to sail back to Haifa. Despite the heat, the crowding, shortage of food and impossible sanitary conditions, especially the struggle for young children and babies – all Holocaust survivors, they were determined to leave the boat only on the shores of their homeland.

The French government refused to help the British force the Jews off the boat. This pitiful situation affected the French people and the entire world. Journalists from every country gathered in Marseilles to cover the story. French and Jewish organizations tried to bring food and clothing to the hostages, but the British would not allow delivery of these basic necessities. A wave of extremely hot July days dominated the south of France that year, making conditions on the boat unbearable. The stench of garbage and human waste filled the air. Shortage of water prevented the Maapilim from bathing. In this suffocating heat people lay half naked on iron floors on the boat, surrounded by high fences of concertina razor wire, as if they might escape and swim away to penetrate the guarded shores of their Holy Land.

The British believed that the Maapilim could be starved into surrender. They should have known better. The subjugating difficulties only encouraged the oppressed passengers. They founded a "floating school" for the 350 children aboard the *Exodus* and taught them Hebrew and Jewish studies.

Eventually, the French government ordered the British to sail the *Exodus* away from its territorial waters within three days. The prison boat with its survivors was sent to Germany, arriving on a foggy dark night. After four weeks of torment, the boat approached Hamburg, and the Maapilim gathered at the wire fences surrounding the decks. As one, they broke into the rallying song Jewish Partisans sang in the Warsaw Ghetto. *This won't be our last way. The day we strived and longed for will soon come. Then we shall announce our presence forever here...*

The scene was ghostly. Scraps of destroyers floated in

the oil-slick harbor. Beak-like bows and shattered masts carried the Nazi Swastika. *Exodus* prisoners were forcibly taken off the boat and transported to former Nazi camps that were used at that time by the British Army as refugee camps.

In Germany many of the Maapilim did not give up but repeated their attempt to migrate to Palestine. They re-boarded the *Exodus*. Some succeeded while others were caught and thrown, by the British into prison or deported to a refugee camp in Cyprus.

Cyprus Detainee Camp

Cyprus internment camps were run by the British government for internment Jews who had attempted to immigrate to Mandatory Palestine in violation of British policy. The camps operated from August 13, 1946 to February 10, 1949, and in total held 53,510 internees. The British government hoped that this deterrent would put an end to Jewish immigration. But before long the British came to realize that detention was not achieving the desired aim. The would-be immigrants continued their attempts to reach Palestine despite violent clashes with British troops and by ragged boats they escaped to the seashores of their Holy Land. The British Army in Cyprus handled the camps according to the rules applicable to prisoner-of-war camps. The detainees were housed in tents. Conditions in the camp were quite harsh, especially for mothers of children and babies. The tents and barracks were overcrowded. There was no privacy and families had no share accommodations with other people. There were no partitions, no lighting fixtures, and no furniture except beds. The food supplied by the British Army was of poor quality. The detainees also suffered from a lack of clothing and shoes. The insufficient water supply, particularly in the hot summers, caused unsanitary conditions and led to skin diseases and infections.

In April 1947, Leibl escaped the Cyprus camp, boarded a fisherman vessel that smuggled him to the shore of Haifa. Upon arrival to the Land of Israel, he was recruited to the Haganah underground – an organization that was established in 1920 to fight against the Arabs in Palestine, and later when the British Mandate was formed (1920 until 1947) they fought to withdraw them from the Land of Israel.

In 1947, the Jews living in Eretz Israel were attacked by five Arab nations: Lebanon, Syria, Jordan, Egypt and Iraq. And so broke the War of Independence. On May 14, 1948 Israel became a state and declared its independence.

The Haganah organization became the Israel Defense Force. Leibl was conscripted to the army and fought the war in the Galilei region. He served in the IDF for 25 years and in 1975 with the rank of major he retired from the service.

CHAPTER 16

My Friend Naima

As the wheels of the El Al airplane kissed the asphalt runway at Ben Gurion Airport, Naima pressed her forehead and squashed her nose against the window. Open-mouthed, she took in her first sight of Israel. Naima was seven years old, her black hair parted to the side, revealing her long neck, her almond eyes and the thick lashes that shaded them. In the dim light of the passenger compartment, she appeared well looked after. Naima's gaze was piercing, revealing something of the turmoil in her heart, the fear and pain of being torn from her home, where she had lived right up until that moment. As the plane turned, Naima saw a panoramic view of the airport. On the left was a tall, round tower whose glass windows were swallowed up by the bright blue of the sky that spring of 1951. Beyond the airplane window,

Naima saw the people in the tower communicating with the airplane using signs and signals.

Georgina, Naima's mother, was a heavy woman. Her eyes, sunken into their sockets, scanned the view around the airplane with a combination of amazement and anxiety. Her hair, as black as a crow, was gathered tightly with a golden pin at the nape of her neck. Impatient, she sat beside her daughter, struggling against the crowding of the plane. But her longing to move to the Holy Land, which they had spoken of so often in their home, gave her the hope and the strength she needed to gather her family and make this arduous journey.

While the passengers were still seated in the belly of the plane on that hot May day, the clerk from the agency arrived along with a group of young men who began to help the passengers descend the stairs off the plane. After a crowded three-hour flight, Operation Ezra and Nehemiah[1] brought one hundred and fifty thousand im-

---

1 The mission was also called Operation Babylon. Ezra and Nehemiah were the leaders who led the Jews from exile from Babylon (present-day Iraq) to Israel. After many years during which Iraq banned its Jews from leaving the country, it allowed them to leave in the 1950s.

migrants from Baghdad to Israel. Their eyes were still scanning their surroundings with wonder and concern when they saw the three trucks covered with muddy gray tarps, as though they had only just returned from the battlefield, waiting to transport them.

Naima and her family members got onto one of the trucks and sat down on the long wooden benches along its length. The tarp material that wrapped around the truck was rolled up and tied to an iron pole, and the passengers could see the landscape of Israel for the first time. The truck began its journey and passed by a series of plantations in bloom. Naima breathed in the sweet, intoxicating scent of orange, grapefruit and clementine blossoms. In a field of wheat by the road, laborers worked harvesting the crops, stacking them into square heaps of hay, until they looked like straw blocks scattered for miles across the fields.

The monotonous shaking of the truck put Naima to sleep, but when it turned off the asphalt road onto an unpaved road, its wheels crunched over gravel and dust rose to her nose and mouth. She woke up from her troubled sleep. Suddenly she saw a view of rocky terrain spotted with hundreds of tents.

"Where have we arrived to?" Naima asked sleepily.

"Soon we will get to the home that has been designated for us," her mother tried to calm her. "We will live there for some time until they find us a permanent place."

Naima was quiet. How could she resist a place she knew nothing about?

The truck arrived and came to a stop. "This is the Gil Amal Magdiel transit camp," announced the representative from the Jewish Agency. "You will live here for some time until your permanent home is established," he encouraged them.

The truck immediately erupted in commotion. People were shouting at the agency officials, the driver, and one another. "We left our beautiful, spacious homes behind in Baghdad, we gave up our professions and the high quality of life that we had up until now. And for what? Just to immigrate, to move to the Holy Land, to live in sand dunes scattered with old tents? Is this the welcome that we deserve?"

"We will get down here," said Yosef, a strong young man, standing by the opening of the truck. With his muscular arms he blocked the other passengers' exit, pushed the confused agency clerk and asked for an immediate solution for their living quarters. The clerk was stunned, unable to speak, as if possessed.

The rest of the new immigrants remained seated on the truck's wooden benches, refusing to get down. Meanwhile, night fell and there were no adequate sleeping arrangements for them, but they were determined not to go to the tents that had been prepared for them.

Suddenly a short, dark young man appeared, his black curls gathered in a rubber band. From underneath the faded bucket hat that he wore, long strands of hair emerged and flew about his face in the wind. His eyes darted around in their sockets, quickly surveying his community, hoping to find some members of his family among them. His white shirt was darkened with sweat stains. He pulled a white kerchief from his pocket, wiped it across his face and forehead, wiping away the sweat of his efforts. The man, who had come to Israel from Iraq not long before, and thus spoke the language of the immigrants, now held a senior position in the Jewish Agency which believed in the mass immigration which befell the young state. Shlomo Hillel was desperately and unwaveringly making a great effort for his people. He worked hard to improve the conditions of the first two hundred immigrants who had left Baghdad. He knew that if he promised to provide them with better housing, they would give in to the agency officials, get off the trucks and be willing to spend the night, on a temporary basis, in the tents where they found themselves.

Shlomo Hillel had the necessary leadership skills and the trust of the new immigrants. He promised that he would not rest until he had visited all the institutions and important persons of the young state to secure permanent housing for them. His words softened the immigrants' resistance. They were moved by his pleas and one after the other they unpacked their belongings and took their place in the designated tent. They were sure that Shlomo Hillel would do everything needed to find them permanent housing right away.

One morning the school principal entered the second-grade class with a dark little girl behind her, her thick black hair hiding most of her face. From underneath her hair, Naima looked shyly out at the children sitting in exemplary order behind their desks. The principal introduced her to us. Nervous, she hid behind her bulky jacket. Her long eyelashes covered her black eyes which scanned the children before her in embarrassment. She did not speak, but her eyes looked around the room where she found herself. Naima was different than the rest of us, the children of survivors from Europe, and this inspired my curiosity. I raised my finger toward the teacher and asked that the new girl sit in the extra chair by my desk. The teacher agreed happily, and Naima joined me. When I asked her who she was and where she had come from, she dropped her chin and shook her head in reply, conveying that she did not understand the words I was saying. "Never mind," I encouraged her, "soon enough you will learn the language and you will be one of us. All of us here are new immigrants from different countries and we learned the language together without too much difficulty." I looked at her little feet. She was wearing high shoes with clumps of mud on their soles. I understood that Naima had come to us from the transit camp. I made it my mission to help make her transition easier and a strong friendship was born between us that developed and went on for many years.

While at my house, Dad planted fruit trees, built a chicken coop, set up a small farm to meet our immediate needs and prepared the land so we, the children, could cultivate our acre for vegetables and flowers, while the vegetables sprouted above the soil and the flowers gave off a pleasant scent — Naima went on shuffling through the sands of the transit camp.

Shlomo Hillel didn't forget his promise and spent days and nights with the ministers of the Mapai who managed every aspect of the state. A year later, he had the transit camp liquidated and relocated its residents to permanent buildings. So our moshav, Magdiel, was home to Jews from Europe alongside those who came from Operation Ezra and Nehemiah, the different Diaspora communities grouped together but apart.

CHAPTER 17

Austerity — Everyone is Hungry

In its first years, the population of Israel numbered around 650,000 people. We were among the 400,000 new immigrants that had left Europe after the Holocaust and along with the mass wave of immigration from the Arab nations (around 300,000 people) and within four years, the population doubled. The steady stream of immigration depleted the country's meager treasury. In order to restrain private consumption, and in the interest of defense funding and development spending, a policy of economic austerity was declared. Distribution of goods and essential services were rationed and supervised. Between 1949 and 1953, the government, headed by David Ben Gurion, issued regulations which, along with the challenges of immigration, made our lives difficult. Likewise, there was a need to instill among the more 'veteran' citizens of our young society (those who immigrated at the end of the previous century or before Israel became independent) the values of solidarity with us — the new immigrants — and not only because of our years of suffering through the Holocaust. The austerity regime applied to everything. Doctor Dov Yosef (Bernard Joseph), a lawyer who served as the military governor of Jerusalem during the War of Independence siege on Jerusalem, was appointed Minister of Austerity and Rations. He imposed rations on food, clothing, and other essential commodities. He determined what we could eat and wear, as well as the style and conditions of our lives.

A diet regime was forced on those immigrants who only several years earlier had suffered the terrible hunger of the Holocaust. Food portions were allocated and purchased with coupons from booklets printed at the Austerity Headquarters, which controlled and oversaw our needs. The weekly amount per person consisted of 60 grams of flour, 17 grams of rice, 20 grams of noodles, 200 grams of cheese, 600 grams of onion and 5 grams of biscuits. The meat ratio was 75 grams per person per month. Even eggs were divided. The most common dark bread was cheap and its rations were unlimited. It was made from whole wheat and of higher nutritional value than white bread. Soon there was a shortage of the whole wheat flour and the country was forced to import wheat from the United States. Nowadays such bread is valued for its healthy ingredients by those who are concerned with the quality of food on their table. Brown sugar was also considered cheap and less desirable by the state's middle-class citizens while today is seen as a healthier choice.

There were citrus fruits in abundance. An orange alongside dark bread, spread with margarine and a little brown sugar or jam was a delicacy. There was little selection of products, but the Jewish mind came up with its own inventions. Against the austerity background, 'alternative' products appeared. Chicory was a cheap substitute for coffee. When we mixed it in boiling water it produced a coarse pulp consisting of granules that got stuck between our teeth. The milk was powdery and its taste bland. A yellowish powder immersed in water was an egg-substitute that gave us a small dose of protein. Ads showed a chicken with the slogan: "the only difference between fresh and dry eggs is the price and the shell." They also offered the recipe: "Two tablespoons of egg powder and two tablespoons of water = 1 egg." When Dov Yosef heard of the "Columbus Egg," he asked if it was possible to turn it into powder. My mother would make my school sandwiches with "wooden" cheese, which got its name for its lean, savory flavor and hardness.

In the bathroom, we raised chicks whose disgusting smell ruined my appetite for the rationed chicken dishes. The mixture of wheat, barley and legumes for bird feed were unavailable, so my mother fattened the chickens on our leftovers and the abundant dark bread. When the chicks grew, they produced bland chicken meat with little nutritional value. The eggs that the chickens laid upgraded our meals, but we shared them with our friends in Tel Aviv, where the shortage was even greater. We also raised pigeons in our yard and their meat was considered a delicacy among poultry. There was plenty of spinach which we found repulsive and would find excuses not to eat.

Mama kept carp swimming in the bathtub which she would kill with a blow of a hammer to their heads, to turn them into Shabbat gefilte fish. The fish fillets' pungent smells filled our house and provided a dose of iodine to our menu. We bought our rationed meals with the coupon booklets that were distributed to families to monitor our consumption. In order to be so lucky as to buy controlled products, Mama would stand in the long line which extended from the opening of the grocery store. The prolonged standing made the veins in her legs swell, and sometimes for nothing, as necessary items such as meat often ran out before her turn came. It was said that in Russia the lines for meat were so long that people would wait for hours until it ran out and then they received cabbage instead.

To keep food cold, we were allotted a quarter of a block of ice, so as "not to drive up the electricity," for those who did not yet own a refrigerator. "Ice, ice," sang the seller from the streets of the transit camp, but before it reached the fridge it had melted completely away. Oil was also divided up and used for heating and cooking, always with that repulsive, stifling smell.

There were also the fashions in clothing called "Lakol" (for all) or "Ata." These products were also paid for with the coupons. The annual budget for adult clothing was

85 points and 45 points for shoes. Later the budget increased to 100 and 50, respectively. In exchange for these points, a man could acquire a short winter coat of coarse wool, short khaki pants, a khaki shirt, a pair of cotton socks and a summer and winter undershirt. The total for those items was 58 points. A woman, for the same number of points, could 'treat herself' to a cotton skirt, cotton dress, viscose shirt, summer socks and fake silk stockings. I remember that in Magdiel, where we moved at the end of the 'trial' period in the transit camp, there were sewing workshops in which women patched "silk" socks that unraveled. When a woman asked Prime Minister David Ben Gurion if her clothing budget also included a wedding dress, he replied: "According to Jewish law, you can get married in the dress you are wearing right now. But when you get pregnant, you will get 70 additional points."

Governmental signs asked the citizens: "Do we ration our clothing or ration immigration?" There were also ideological clichés: "Our sons didn't give their lives for the war of abundance." There was a big price gap between the rationed products and those that any ordinary citizen might purchase without points, since price was determined by the seller. A caricature showed a man and woman standing before the shop window of a clothing store, the man seeing only the price tags while the woman fantasized that she herself was wearing the luxurious clothes. The Mikolinsky shoe store featured a selection of shoes "for all" alongside higher quality products. The General Zionists Party, which opposed the Mapai government's austerity regime, posted ads showing a family in which the husband wears a suit but goes barefoot, the wife wears a skirt and only a bra on her upper half, the girl wears a little undershirt without so much as a skirt to cover her bottom half, and the boy wears just a pair of underpants. Member of Parliament, Raziel Naor, said that on behalf of liberty that "we went without shoes." There was a common joke about a boy who walked taking big steps because he didn't want to ruin his shoes.

Fashions were essentially modest. Women's tailored suits, like those of the men, were the fashion of choice. Women remade old clothes, patched socks, and took hemlines in or out according to their needs. In the dresses I wore at that time, the seamstress left a large fold of extra fabric so that she could extend the skirt as I grew. Clothes that faded were dyed again and would stain the other clothes when first washed. My aunts and grandfather who had emigrated to the United States, concerned themselves with our shortages and sent us packages of everything we might need. When such a package arrived, my two-year-old sister and myself, four years old, would dance happily and call out in merry Polish: "Pichke from America!" (A package from America). My dresses were not bought in a store but designed by my mother from cloth in boring colors that she chose. In the packages that arrived from America, Mama received fabulous dresses with daring décolletage which went against the norms of modesty. She would take them to a dressmaker who would give them a more proper look. Coquetry was considered inappropriate for women. Beauty treatments were frowned upon. Hair dye and makeup were considered breaking the laws of nature. The fashion of necessity produced simple, conservative clothes. In the store, when my mother asked the salesman "how much does a pair of shoes cost?" He answered: "this much with coupons and this much on the black market." I wore my boots until my toes broke through them. Then my mother cut the ends off the shoes and my feet, in their coarse cotton socks, wiggled free. But when this 'trim' was not enough, the shoes were passed down to my little sister, who always felt deprived, complaining that she didn't get a new pair of shoes. Perhaps that is why she became such a well-dressed and beautifully groomed woman later on.

In winter, Dad extended his wide khaki pants by wearing his long underwear, tight all the way down to his ankles, underneath them. For a while he owned a warehouse for animal feed for the auxiliary farms or settlements around the Sharon region. His pants pockets were always full of wheat and barley. When he gave me my allowance, the coins were covered with dust from the grains. Dad always looked dusty to me, carrying the remnants of the mix bags around with him. I prayed he might be a postal clerk, like my friend's father who always wore a white shirt.

The textile factory "Ata" was beside Yeruham and provided employment to people who lived in the South. When it closed in the 1960s, it caused social protests from the southern development towns, many of whom were among the great number of unemployed at that time.

Under the supervision of the austerity authorities, "Ata" used cheap raw materials and manufactured low-quality products, including uniform khaki-colored work clothes and men's underwear made from coarse cotton. There were also other fashion establishments such as Lodzia and Gottex that mainly produced underwear. The latter was established by a Mrs. Gottlieb, who would sell her wares door-to-door, until she became a designer, manufacturer and exporter of fashionable swimwear "Gottex" and the world's best-known Israeli textile manufacturer.

On Egged's "Sasson" buses, our sweaty bodies crowded together, pressed against one another. In order to alert the driver to stop at the station, we would pull on a plastic cord that hung from the ceiling and which was always torn, preventing it from ringing to alert the driver to stop. Due to the commotion, the driver never heard the signal and would keep driving past the station. So, passengers would burst out shouting in protest, "Wait, wait!" The bus never closed its windows, letting all the hot air inside in the summer, and the cold air in all winter. To get off the bus you had to pull firmly on the back-door handle which opened like an accordion. As it was a narrow passage for someone to pass, passengers clung to each other and the small skirmishes that resulted were sometimes violent. Several of the buses had back doors. If you managed to make your way onto the crowded bus, you almost certainly would have no way of getting off it. The bodies squashed together, and I often had to inhale the smell of dank sweat from unwashed bodies.

On the bus it was every man for himself. Endless fights broke out over seats. It was enough for a passenger to signal with his hands that he would be getting off at the nearest station for other passengers to hover over his soon-to-be-vacated seat, making it hard to get off. Nobody bothered to stand up to let a pregnant woman or elderly person sit. My sister and I were educated in Polish manners. If it reached my parents' ears that we had not gotten up, out of respect, to give up our seat for someone older, we would be punished. But my mother only kept up her cultural values so long as they suited her. Bus fare was subsidized and was affordable to all. Any child over five years old had to pay. Despite my mother's manners, she tried to avoid buying a ticket for me and would tell the driver that I was only four. I would get very angry with her for diminishing me and correct her mistake. I don't know if she got angry because I embarrassed her or because she had to pay the difference.

Sometimes we would wait at the bus stop for hours in the sun and humidity. Buses packed full with passengers would pass right by us without stopping. The frustrated waiting passengers would run after the bus and curse the driver. The 'sprinters' sometimes displayed so much fortitude that they could run after it all the way to their destination. There were also those who hung off the ladder on the back of the bus. People hung onto the rungs as though they were drowning and that was their lifeline. There were also the athletic types who managed in this way to ride on the roof of the bus, which was fenced with rods designed to store passengers' belongings. Accidents must have been caused by these acrobatics, but they were negligible.

On more than one occasion I was lucky enough to sit in a seat beside the window. Once a man sat beside me and pressed up against my body. I shrunk, and tried to lean against the window, reducing myself to make space for him, but he kept pushing, making his way to my hidden places. I was either embarrassed or did not understand his intentions, and did not make a big fuss as I should have done. I tried to give up my seat for him and get up, but then he was on top of me, rubbing up against me with his knees. When a passenger sitting beside the window got up, his neighbor who sat in the aisle seat, did not bother to get up to make way for him, as such a gesture would have cost him his own seat, what with the other passengers already eying the vacancy like vultures. When minibuses taxis finally entered the scene, most of us did not have the fare that they demanded.

At the Magdiel cinema, my friends and I would go to children's movies or those that were not limited to adult audiences. At the entrance we would buy 20 grams of sunflower seeds, roasted and salted, that were sold in cones made of newspaper. We developed great skill at cracking open the shells and spitting them on the concrete floor of the movie theater, as did the rest of the audience. The organic matter served as a carpet spread across the cold floor. The translation, never synchronized, rolled to the right side of the screen, making a disharmony between the voices and the movements of the actors' lips. I made an effort to understand what was happening on the screen from the actors' lip movements, which was how I began to learn English. Sometimes the technician screened the wrong movie from the back of the hall. When the reel tape ran out, he had to take a break to set up the next reel. People in the audience, sitting in the dark, would whistle and complain about the lag and his lack of skill. Many times, the power went out and the whole theater went completely dark. In one screening, when I was only four years old, the lights went out. Beside me was a soldier, about 18 years old, whom I knew as my neighbor from Magdiel. The extended darkness scared me and I burst into tears. The soldier comforted me, pulling me from my seat and sat me on his knees, trying to calm me down. When the film was over, he held my hand all the way home as I walked alongside my friends. When one of my friends reported what had happened in the movie theater, my parents panicked and whisked me off to the family doctor. The doctor rolled up my dress and used his fat fingers to check if my virginity was still intact after the incident. The trauma of that examination still reminds me of the shame I felt that day.

During the summer break from school, a Greenberg truck driver drove us to the Herzliya seaside. When we saw the clear turquoise waters of the Mediterranean, we jumped with joy on the benches, crying "here's the sea, here's the sea!" 'Gazoz,' a bubbling soft drink with raspberry or lemon flavors, was sold at seafront kiosks, until it was replaced by the seltzer bottle that Mama brought along to save a few pennies. "Bagels, bagels!" An old woman loaded with her wares announced. "Corn on the cob, corn on the cob!" Corn was also sold on the beach from a big, hot aluminum tub that had just been taken off the coals.

For Mama, the seaside meant "nutritional food." She claimed that the seawater, with all its salt, would stimulate her skinny daughter's appetite. She would fill a cooler with sandwiches full of butter for my sister and I. If I finished eating without complaint, I would get a lemon or raspberry popsicle. When I went into the waves, my mother, the hem of her dress pulled to her knees, would stand watching me like a hawk, her feet in the water, letting me drift between the waves beyond her control. She only allowed me to go into the water up to my waist. But I loved catching the waves, letting them buoy me, free from her control, into the depths. So, Mom would come closer, her dress wet, its hem soaked, and pull me out. Events like this would always end in punishment. Mom would sit me on the armchair, made of plastic fabric, its upper edges fixed with nails to the wooden structure supporting it, which stung my bare body. Then she wrapped me up in a towel and vigorously dried every centimeter of my body lest I get cold. The wet towel, full of sand, scraped the skin of my face and body and tears stung my flesh. I sat like that until the truck came back and took us all home.

There was also a swimming pool in the nearby Ramot Hashavim town. We would ride our bicycles, pedaling uphill in the heat for the chance to get into the refreshing water. All of my friends took swimming lessons, but I wasn't allowed to out of concern that if I learned to swim, I would drown in the pool. There was nothing to do but sit on the side of the pool and imitate my friends' leg movements. And so, I learned to swim. Maybe that's why I love swimming the most of all the sports.

The austerity headquarters established a way to monitor traders and manufacturers. Police and inspectors were authorized to investigate anyone, to treat him as a criminal and to confiscate his coupon books. Inspectors, who wore a green ribbon on their arms — "supervised"

— sunk so low as to inspect the bags of passengers on the bus. There, under their clothes, the passengers hid food products and poultry that they had bought from farms or kibbutzs where the austerity measures were not felt as intensely. To mislead inspectors, passengers would start shouting *"kwa, kwa"* like a goose or duck and so protected their friends who hid the forbidden poultry. Our friend Leibl Frost, who lived in Givat Hashlosha kibbutz, always made sure to provide for us to cover our shortages. Bunches of green bananas would find a place under the kitchen sink, where they stayed until they ripened.

The government ministers who were entrusted with administration of the state did so insufficiently. The austerity regime created the black market. Dollar changers became so common that they did their trade on the street corners of Lilienblum-Allenby in Tel Aviv, like street-walkers in broad daylight. They would spit on their fingertips to wet the green bills and speed the pace of their counting before the police could catch them. When the police showed up, they would run, frightened, and take refuge with the divine spirit at the Great Synagogue on Allenby Street. Austerity created terrible inflation. With the green bills that our relatives had sent us in their packages from America, my father would run to buy groceries for fear of prices rising even more. However, the severe shortage of products made it hard to waste money.

An industry of austerity jokes expressed the public's cynicism. In election propaganda pamphlets, there were cartoons showing women making small talk: "I heard about some Dr. Yosef who invented an effective medicine against the modern sector." The austerity edicts were bitterly referred to as the "Holocaust survivors' diet". They said of Dov Yosef that when he entered a workers' restaurant, he greeted its guests with a "bon appetite" and they answered, "We have appetites, thank God, but unfortunately there is no food." Songs and jokes mainly dealt with the miserliness of the austerity minister. It was said that one day he returned home for lunch. His wife served a jar which contained *a* cool white substance. "What's that?" He asked. "It's leben, a new product from Tnuva," she answered with pride. "Delicious," he admitted reluctantly. "Tomorrow I will list it among the controlled products." New slang also crept in. "Austerity face," "Tzena Face" was a term for an unappealing girl.

The social protest, which was not long in coming, could not have been prevented by the austerity minister. In July of 1950, merchants went on a general strike and the homemakers' protest followed. In the spontaneous partisan war that broke out, the Women's Organization for Consumer Protection was founded. It was a war of the women who had lost faith in the policy-making experts regarding their children's diets. "We cannot raise our children without apples, bananas, meat or milk."

The press took advantage of the government's struggle and highlighted the gap between what they had promised and what they had implemented. In 1949, Carlebach wrote in his article in the newspaper, 'Maariv': "The citizen feels that he is not only just a cog in the machine of the apparatus, but that he is an interference which disturbs the regular working of things. What a sorry development that the citizen feels like a criminal."

The newspaper 'Davar,' the mouthpiece for the Mapai establishment, represented the administration and explained the wisdom of austerity. It attacked the traders and industrialists who, they argued, were at fault for the most shameful chapter in the history of Israel's Jewish population for raising product prices in order to sell them on the black market. The newspaper saw itself as having to take up the burden of fighting the war on the black market and exposing corruption. "There's no austerity, no supervision, there's debauchery and it undermines the government's authority," the paper argued.

In his book "Operation Babylon," Shlomo Hillel, who had been Minister of Police for a time, wrote how, despite the scarcity of resources, he decided to bring the Jews of Iraq to Israel in 1950. He tells the story of Shkolnik and Pinchas Sapir, then minister of finance, trying to thwart their arrival. In his memoir, Hillel recounts the words of Levi Eshkol: "Wait patiently. Tell the Jews that they will come but not to hurry. We don't have the capacity to take them in now. We don't even have tents. If they come, they will have to live in the street. You have to make it clear to them, otherwise they will be resentful, and rightly so. I don't want them to show up at my house. I'll bring them to you, to the Maagan Michael Kibbutz". But when Hillel raised the issue to David Ben Gurion, the prime minister said: "Young man, I heard that you are going to Baghdad to bring Jews. Tell them to come and come quick! What might happen if the Iraqis suddenly change their minds and cancel your agreement (to allow the Jews to leave)?

Go and bring them back quickly. God speed."

In the black market, corruption and fraud became common practice. I saw Dad buy food coupons from people I didn't know more than once. Sometimes, when Mom bought a product in high demand that was on the ration list, the merchant forced her to buy additional products beyond what was allotted to us, as a condition of selling her the permitted product. The black market thrived. By February 1950, there were already 500 cases against citizens who were involved in it. But the law that was meant to enforce it was largely unresponsive. A poster from the ministry of rationing showed a choked snake with the caption: "Eliminate the black market and it won't eliminate you," but supervision was a failure and law enforcement unable to follow up on everything.

In 1955, as the stream of new immigrants slowed and the German government began to pay reparations to victims of the Holocaust, our economic situation improved and the state coffers were filled with funds that the Germans sent the survivors, marking the end of the coupon system. Dad refused to stand before the committees that determined the survivors' eligibility. "I don't want any part of this, I can't dredge up any memories. There is no compensation for what the Nazis did to us." Mom, on the other hand, turned up for every possible commission and claimed what she deserved.

I remember the austerity period from my childhood, between ages four and eight, mainly as it concerned my mother's daily difficulties in obtaining food, standing with her in long queues that went all the way from the shop to our house, and the guilt that she made me feel — a skinny girl refusing to eat what her mother had gone to such lengths to procure. "There are children who had nothing to eat during the Holocaust and you are refusing to eat the banana?" She protested.

CHAPTER 18

A Glance Back in Anger

My childhood home was in the Gil Amal neighborhood of Magdiel, in the heart of the Sharon region, erected on the ruins of Biyar 'Adas, the Arab village that we conquered in the War of Independence. The village's Arab residents moved beyond the Jordan river where they remain to this day. In 1950, there were already some 50 new duplex housing projects scattered there. From the top of the hill, our neighborhood looked like a bowl of peas roasting in the Sahara heat. Unpaved, no infrastructure, the settlement was built on top of swamps that had not yet been dried out, swarming with mosquitos. It was all ready to give the new immigrants a warm welcome.

In the front yard of our house my father planted a tree that was meant to yield pears, but by mistake he planted avocado, something that we, from cold Poland, were unfamiliar with. The tree grew very tall, spread its branches and bore ripe fruit that never made it to our table. The fruit fell and rotted, fertilizing the tree's roots.

A loquat tree was also planted by accident, but since it grew beside the fence, children would happily pick the ripe fruits on their way to school. Olives too were not in my parents' culinary repertoire. They never managed to haul them out of their jar with a fork or knife. I used both my fingers and showed them how to "fish" for the slippery delicacies.

The Egged bus that connected us to our capital, Ramatayim, came through only rarely. The driver, Reuben, unlike us, was a native of the land. He hated children, refugees, the noise passengers made and would eject anyone from the bus that disturbed his peace.

The state was established by Ashkenazi Jews without much consideration for the Mizrahi[2] Jews. I will never understand the shortsighted memory of the immigrants from Europe. Not five years earlier they themselves stood on the verge of anti-Semitic annihilation, but those

---

2   Jews from those diaspora communities in North Africa and the Middle East (as opposed to Europe)

who survived deemed it right to feel superior to those other, darker Diaspora Jews. A social and economic gap widened between the immigrants. Ethnic injustice and discrimination began to emerge. Their eastern culture was not valued or appreciated. The teachers in schools were mostly of European extraction and they imparted their culture and disastrous history even to those who had suffered painful histories of their own, in non-European countries of origin. Most of the Ashkenazis lived in duplexes built on a half-dunam plot of land, while those who were less fortunate, by virtue of birthplace and history, went on living in the tents that stood in the Gil Amal encampment. Eventually tin shacks were built for them and about a year and a half later, they were moved to their permanent homes.

Our family lived alongside another Polish family — the Kulenders. We shared our allotted plot of land with them including the yard that was used for children's play and the adults' social life. The field was worked, planted, sown and even served as an auxiliary farm where we raised chickens, geese and other poultry. Soon Mom grew close with the neighbor Pnina, and they both used to cook together in the same kitchen. Despite the closeness, as was customary of Polish etiquette, neither addressed the other by her first name. "Mrs. Neighbor" was their mutual address. Mrs. Neighbor and her husband Yeruham had two sons: Aharon, my little sister's age, and little Yodeleh. Aharon would slap Rachela and I would get him back. Afterward, my father would punish me with a slap as Yeruham would Aharon. One day, enraged by the children's disputes, a loud quarrel broke out between the two mothers. From then on, the women quarreled constantly. A barbed-wire fence was built dividing the lot into equal halves, and quiet returned to the yard. The neighborhood's other inhabitants, irrespective of where they came from, were shocked by this development but unable to take a stance on the strife. Ultimately, the Kulender family moved to a shared house in Ramat Gan. With their move, our mother became gentler and the relations between the two women regained its old tenderness. Each woman began to miss her friend. My sister and I were lucky to join Mom on more than one visit to Pnina. It required transferring on three buses until we arrived at the home of the woman who was no longer Mrs. Neighbor. I don't remember what the women came to call each other, since the nickname no longer fit the present circumstances. My sister and I also grew close with Aharon, as they no longer maintained the heat of battle that kept their discord alive.

The Elishama moshav, which bordered our neighborhood, was inhabited by Libyan immigrants. Those Mizrahi boys were strong, tanned and handsome. They worked the land of their settlement and honorably supported their parents who never managed to adapt to the Ashkenazi-dominated country. When I began to show signs of growing up, my parents indicated the "right" boys for me and forbade me to develop romantic relationships with those of Mizrahi origins. Dad kept close watch on the traffic of my suitors and banned me from socializing with those who came from outside the moshav. "Who's he, who's he?" Mom used to ask about any young man that came to our doorstep.

"Whoozeehoozee?" My sister and I imitated her accent.

In any case, I went horseback riding with those young men among the orchards and the wheat and barley fields. Together we picked anemones, daffodils and cyclamen flowers between the old railroad tracks. When I returned home after wonderful hours spent in Elishama, my arms full of wildflowers, it was proof that I had crossed the permitted line and had spent my time in the forbidden moshav.

Thanks to those guys, I became acquainted with the spicy foods of the Tripolitans or their neighboring Moroccans. From them I learned that fish was not necessarily gefilte fish, and that when it was seasoned and served in the North African fashion, it was called "chraime". On Friday evenings, the neighborhood filled with the mix of scents that wafted from the delicacies of the various kitchens from different backgrounds. The flavors of Hungarian goulash, the Romanian ciorba, and the Yemenite *schug* (hot sauce), emitted from the kitchens of various housewives. I never understood how the Iraqi mothers were able to make those perfect, crispy *kubbes*, with the ground, spiced, perfectly tender meat inside.

In the evenings at the Magdiel Cinema, we cracked open sunflower seeds sold in a newspaper cone. The boys escorted us home from the evening's entertainment. In their company we were not afraid of the loud noises from the ice factory. Even the croaking of frogs from the local swamp weren't frightening on warm nights. In the dense eucalyptus grove that bordered the neighborhood, we would walk and get lost with them. How beautiful those endless summer nights were...

On the outskirts of every prestigious Israeli neighborhood, a poor one was established. Savion was next to Ganei Tikvah and Yehud, Caesarea alongside Or Akiva, and Neve Monosson beside Or Yehuda. It appears that the plans of the local authorities ensured that the affluent would have a population affixed to it whose inhabitants could serve as "foreign" workers in their homes.

Michel who worked as a mechanic in the garage in Caesarea, came from Or Akiva. I met him on a family vacation that we spent on the Caesarea beach. Although he was born in Morocco, he looked like an Ashkenazi angel. His blue eyes and blond hair, which waved as he flew down the road on his Vespa, did not even raise the slightest suspicion in me that he belonged to the "wrong" ethnicity.

Under this camouflage, I could invite him over. But Dad had more developed senses. It was impossible to fool him. Michel drove two hours on the old Haifa-Tel Aviv road to show up for the date that we had set but my father, without my knowing, did not allow him in, and when Michel arrived to our doorstep, Dad instructed him to go back the way he had come. I never understood why my suitors were disappointing me, never showing up for our dates.

Rivka and Pesach Segal

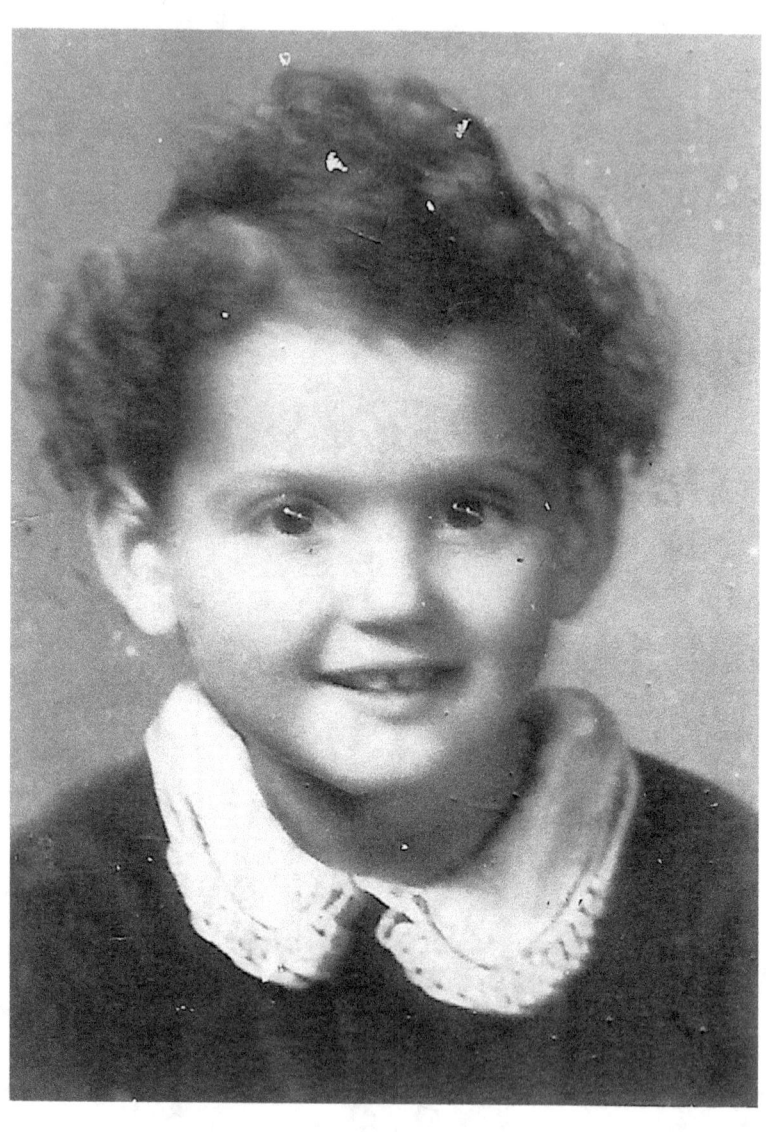

Sarah Segal

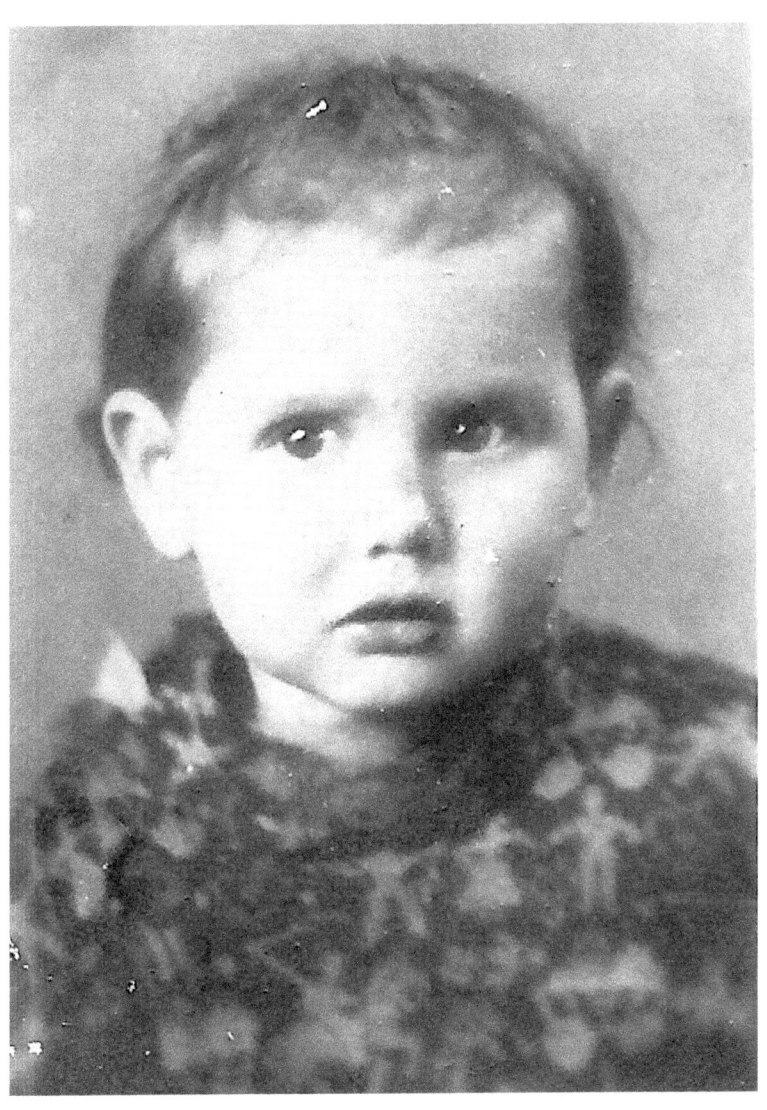

Rachel Shauli

The Segal Family

Pesach Segal - Bottom row, First from the right

Maj. Sarah in the IDF

Sarah

www.ingramcontent.com/pod-product-compliance
Lightning Source LLC
LaVergne TN
LVHW020426070526
838199LV00004B/302